J.R.R. TOLKIEN

is the creator of that rich and immensely varied fantasy-world, Middle-earth. The compelling vitality of Tolkien's imagination has made him perhaps the most successful contemporary writer of fantasy. Countless readers of all ages have been held by the adventures of Frodo the Hobbit and the Fellowship of the Ring as they struggle against the powerful empire of Sauron, the Evil One.

In **J.R.R. Tolkien,** Robley Evans explores the foundations of Tolkien's art and illuminates the profound moral seriousness of Tolkien's work.

J.R.R. Tolkien is the fourth volume in a series of critical appreciations called *WRITERS FOR THE SEVENTIES*.

WRITERS FOR THE SEVENTIES
J.R.R. Tolkien

WRITERS FOR THE SEVENTIES

Kurt Vonnegut, Jr. by Peter J. Reed

Richard Brautigan by Terence Malley

Hermann Hesse by Edwin F. Casebeer

J.R.R. Tolkien by Robley Evans

General Editor: Terence Malley,
Long Island University

J.R.R. TOLKIEN

by

Robley Evans

Connecticut College

WARNER
PAPERBACK LIBRARY
NEW YORK

WARNER PAPERBACK LIBRARY EDITION
First Printing: December, 1972

ACKNOWLEDGMENTS

From BEOWULF translated by Burton Raffel. Copyright © 1963 by Burton Raffel. Reprinted by arrangement with The New American Library, Inc., New York, New York.

From THE HOBBIT by J .R. R. Tolkien (Copyright 1937 and 1938, by J. R. R. Tolkien). Reprinted by permission of the publisher Houghton Mifflin Company, and of George Allen & Unwin Ltd.

From THE LORD OF THE RINGS by J. R. R. Tolkien (Copyright © 1965 by J. R. R. Tolkien). Reprinted by permission of the publisher Houghton Mifflin Company, and of George Allen & Unwin Ltd.

From TREE AND LEAF by J. R. R. Tolkien (Copyright © 1964 by George Allen & Unwin Ltd.). Reprinted by permission of the publisher Houghton Mifflin Company, and of George Allen & Unwin Ltd.

Warner Paperback Library is a division of Warner Books, Inc., 315 Park Avenue South, New York, N.Y. 10010.

For Jennifer

For I am the daughter of Elrond.

WRITERS FOR THE SEVENTIES
J.R.R. Tolkien

Foreword. J.R.R. Tolkien:

A Writer for the Seventies

J.R.R. Tolkien, by Robley Evans, is one volume in a series of critical appreciations under the collective title "Writers for the Seventies." Other books in this series are *Kurt Vonnegut, Jr.,* by Peter J. Reed; *Richard Brautigan,* by Terence Malley; and *Hermann Hesse,* by Edwin F. Casebeer. The intention of these studies is to provide clear and balanced discussions of the main themes and techniques of the four authors in question. In each case, the critic has avoided excessively technical, academic terminology. In general, the four critics have addressed their subjects directly or even personally, without the sort of detachment that makes so many critical studies seem remote. Hopefully, the volumes in the Writers for the Seventies series will serve as good introductions to the four authors under discussion, for readers only slightly familiar with their books, while offering fresh insights for those who have already read the major works of Tolkien, Vonnegut, Brautigan, and Hesse.

A second—less direct—intention of the Writers for the Seventies series is to help, in a small way, to bridge that large and apparently increasing gap between the high school and college age readers of today and their parents and/or teachers. Each of the critics involved in this project is a youngish professor at an American college. All four are in their thirties: old enough to have had their graduate training in what seems already, only ten or twelve years later, a time of relatively settled, traditional standards; young enough to feel the impact of today's counter culture and to be aware of their students' insistence on "relevance" in literature. In each volume, the emphasis is on critical *appreciation*; in each case, the critic tries to arrive at qualitative judgments about his author's achievement and to define the value of this author for readers of all ages.

But why these four authors in particular? Why Tolkien, Vonnegut, Brautigan, and Hesse? Early in his book, *Future Shock*, Alvin Toffler asserts that "Writers have a harder and harder time keeping up with reality."* And, of course, it is possible that the "reality" captured by these four writers will soon cease to hold the attention of readers, that each of the four will soon be seen as someone who had a certain vogue in the late-1960s and early-1970s and then faded off the bookstore racks and out of the minds of readers. This is possible, but not, I think, probable. Despite the vagaries of taste and popularity, the strange chemistry that makes today's best seller next year's remainder item, it seems likely that all four authors focused upon in the Writers for the Seventies series will continue to hold the attention of American readers, particularly younger readers of high school and college ages.

Needless to say, the four authors are very different: Hesse, the pacifist, deep in Eastern religions and Jungian

*New York: Bantam Books, 1971, p.5.

psychology; Tolkien, the Oxford don, absorbed in medieval literature and philology; Vonnegut, the former PR man turned satirist of an increasingly dehumanized America; Brautigan, that transitional figure between the Beat Generation and the Hippies, concerned with a gentle world of trout fishing and green growing things. Indeed, if we were to imagine the four of them in some Paradise of Authors (or—that favorite test-question situation—cast up together on a desert island), we might very well decide that they would have little to say to each other, about their works, about their interests.

Yet, for all their differences, there are some important common denominators running through the works of Hesse, Tolkien, Vonnegut, and Brautigan. Perhaps outlining a few of these will partly explain why all four writers began to attract large audiences in the United States at approximately the same time. First of all, speaking broadly, all four can be described as fantasy-writers. Whether through interior fantasies (like *Steppenwolf* and *In Watermelon Sugar*) or through exterior fantasies (like *The Lord of the Rings* and *The Sirens of Titan*)—all four authors use fantasy to comment on reality. Of course, any successful fantasy (from fairy-tale to science fiction) comments in some way or other on ordinary reality. But our four authors have all, in their very different ways, been able to give their fantasies the sort of internal coherence, plausibility, and substance that enable their readers to suspend disbelief and accept what Coleridge called the "poetic truth" behind fantasy.

In common with virtually every significant writer of the last half-century, the reality behind their fantasies is pretty grim. In all four authors, a war—World War I or World War II—serves as either implicit or explicit background. The appalling catastrophe of the First World War, the slaughter of an entire generation of young men, seems always just beneath the surface of Hesse's major works; in Tolkien, the vast carnage of World War II paralleled exactly the composition of his own version of an ultimate struggle between forces of light and darkness; the Second World War has had the most direct influence on Vonnegut, who was in the war, a POW and a miraculous survivor of the hideous fire-bombing of Dresden; for Brautigan, the youngest of the four authors, World War II is coincident with his earliest conscious memories, and stands ironically as a time of coherence, when things were easier to understand than they could ever be again.

All four authors would surely agree with the "moral" of Vonnegut's *Mother Night*: "We are what we pretend to be, so we must be careful about what we pretend to be." In all four, this bare statement is developed in rich, complex terms. All four are ultimately concerned with self-definition, with the problem of a person's realizing his full humanity (or, in Tolkien's case, I suppose we must also say his full hobbithood). In all four, self-fulfillment is threatened by an essentially dehumanized and dehumanizing world: Hesse's world of vulgar materialism, Tolkien's world in which Sauron aspires to enslave the spirits of all living creatures, Vonnegut's world in which machines often threaten to replace humanity, Brautigan's world of dropouts from a society without sustaining values.

Finally—and perhaps the most important thing Hesse, Tolkien, Vonnegut, and Brautigan have in common—all four authors share an affirmative sense of the possibilities of the human spirit. Without denying the pitfalls that surround their characters, without settling for facile optimism, all four of these Writers for the Seventies show us in their works that there are still things a person can do, that there are still values to be found by looking around oneself and (even more important) by looking *within* oneself. In this time of disillusionment and danger, we need writers like Hesse, Tolkien, Vonnegut, and Brautigan —to remind us that Joy is still possible, to teach us (in Hesse's phrase) how to hear the laughter of the Immortals.

"Don't adventures ever have an end?" wonders Sam, early in *The Lord of the Rings*. He immediately answers his own question: "I suppose not. Someone else always has to carry on the story." One of the major triumphs of J.R.R. Tolkien's Trilogy is the sheer size and scope of the adventures narrated. Due to Tolkien's apparently inexhaustible narrative energy, the reader is drawn along irresistibly—often breathlessly—from adventure to adventure, even as the characters are drawn to the end of the Third Age of Middle-earth.

Another—perhaps even greater—triumph of *The Lord of the Rings* is the way Tolkien gives those improbable heroes, the hobbits, such a large share in the "carrying on" of the adventures. Small, peaceful, devoted to creature comforts (to two dinners, when they can get them), hobbits nevertheless show themselves capable of great fortitude and endurance. As Gandalf the Wizard says to Frodo (even as he'd said earlier of Frodo's uncle, Bilbo Baggins), "There is more about you than meets the eye."

In *J.R.R. Tolkien*, Robley Evans describes this hidden (or inner, hobbit-strength as "commitment to a greater vision of life" than oneself. For the victory of the Allies over the powerful, evil forces of Sauron, in which Frodo and Sam play *the* key role, is essentially a victory of the moral imagination. As Evans brings out, this victory of faith and affirmation over sterility and living-death seems particularly relevant in our own age of anti-heroes, in this time when we can readily identify with the small and apparently powerless.

In his emphasis on persistence and on the validity of commitment to one's imaginative vision, Tolkien is a genuinely *inspirational* writer. Although the world of Middle-earth is strange to us and far away in time, we can all respond to Gandalf's words, "Let us now go on with the journey we have begun!"

Terence Malley
Long Island University
Brooklyn, New York

Table of Contents:

Preface.

J.R.R. Tolkien's life has been spent in the British university system where he has studied the ancient languages of Europe, especially those from which modern English is derived. But his chief fame since World War II has come from his works of fantasy. Tolkien's wide appeal in an age when fantasy usually pertains to writers of science fiction might, at first, seem strange. His kind of fantasy—with its elves and hobbits—appears entirely out of place in the century of computers, space capsules, and flea collars. Science and reason would seem, in theory, to have shown man the right way to live, whether he follows their instructions or not. Instead, what we see is dissatisfaction with this brave new world of material improvements and increased power over the natural world. Too often wars and destruction of nature's order have been caused by "reasonable" men, making us distrustful of reason itself. In such conditions, Tolkien's fantasy satisfies our need for purpose in our lives and meaning in the external world. Fantasy, as Tolkien defines it, does this in its own special way, and it touches those elements in our makeup, such as imagination and feeling, which cannot be computed and which, misdirected, can often be destructive. Tolkien sees fantasy as a means of freeing or cleansing us, and turning our "irrational" powers to good account.

Unlike writers of science fiction, Tolkien relies upon the literary traditions of the past as well as upon his imagination as sources for his fantasy. He does not wish to break with Western culture or with the Romantic tradition that knowledge gives us power to change the world for the better. The imagination has enriched us in the past; it can continue to do so, not by throwing out our inheritance but by building upon it, and especially upon its familiar and eternally meaningful myths, symbols and dreams. Furthermore, imagination is a power for good and for action in the real world, not just a tool for escaping reality. In Tolkien's understanding, the fantasist is a storyteller and historian who makes our past valuable by manifesting its power in the present.

This study focuses upon Tolkien's imagined world in *The Hobbit* and *The Lord of the Rings*. It is not concerned with the author's life or with his moral philosophy for itself. Instead, it tries to show how Tolkien creates a believable world in which his ideas assume shapes and commit actions, an imaginative creation which moves us deeply because Tolkien is a good writer as well as a moral visionary. The narrative and the ideas go together. Ultimately, Tolkien is interested in *power*, in ordering the created world in such a way that it illustrates the creation and the uses of power in the reader's world, too. Consequently, this study must examine Tolkien's theories about the nature and form of fantasy; the literary sources and background for his work; and the artful way in which

20

he gives form to the fantastic. *The Lord of the Rings* is a major work of twentieth-century fiction with serious implications for life as we know it. We must describe its literary structure as well as its thematic contents because it is in the conjunction of the two that the power of the imagination is manifest. Tolkien's popularity in recent years has come about not because his fiction provides an "escape" in the usual sense, but because it is a direct and beautifully written commentary on our lives. How this happens will be explained in the pages that follow.

Chapter One: The Enchanter's Power

In describing the present condition of Western European culture, Robert Langbaum bluntly asserts that there is now no "publicly accepted moral and emotional Truth, there are only perspectives toward it—those partial meanings which individuals may get a glimpse of at particular moments." [1] Society at the present time is in a state of fragmentation, without common agreement about standards of morality or the nature of reality. Instead we have only "partial meanings" observed first by one person and then another, and so haphazard in their appearance and so subjective or downright untrustworthy in their presentation that there can be no reliable consensus about their truth. In such a world, contemporary literature often seems only to reflect the uncertainty, alienation, and despair of its readers, and to suggest that there are few or no ultimate truths to be affirmed: Man is alone, helpless and basically passive in a meaningless universe; there is nothing to be done to alter his condition. In such a world, imaginative literature often seems to have rejected its traditional subject matter, its ancient and accepted forms, and its familiar goals, among them the affirmation of "moral and emotional Truth" and the creation of delightful imaginary people and their doings. Samuel Beckett's characters circle grimly around one another, "waiting for Godot," who never comes; the bookstores are filled with the accounts of individuals' efforts to make contact with other human beings, with events in the real world, with themselves.

With such a picture in mind, perhaps the popularity of J.R.R. Tolkien should not surprise us. Tolkien's most important work, *The Lord of the Rings*, not only affirms that "moral and emotional Truth" may be discovered. It also argues that there can be general community agreement about Truth, that this reality can be manifest in the everyday world, and that the imagination, expressing itself through words and stories, can reveal meaning to all men. In his major fiction, Tolkien provides an antidote to present despair by taking us back to the traditional themes and literary conventions of European literature and its mythic sources, not for an escape into the bookish past, but for a return to those values—moral, emotional, imaginative—which produced our greatest literary works in the first place. Such values are not outmoded, or beyond the reach of contemporary man, so long as he possesses imaginative power to realize them in this world.

Tolkien is a Renaissance man whose essentially Christian vision of the universe finds it ordered and purposive with places for all created beings whose relationships in the community of being provide their lives with moral and spiritual meaning. In this vision such ideas as individual responsibility, exercise of human will in choosing between good and evil, fellow-feeling for other creatures, have a positive function. And exactly because Tolkien can

23

define the world as one organized by laws and purposes, he can show that action, too, is possible; men can choose to do good or evil and to make gestures which shape events and the lives of others, for better or worse.

Such a sense of ultimate moral conclusions, of the possibility of "doing something," gives meaning to individual lives in a way that most modern fiction cannot do. Tolkien's emphasis falls upon "function" in defining moral necessities. Furthermore, his vision includes the creative artist as a moral being who orders the world in his imaginative work and thereby expresses that Truth which lies at the source of lives and actions. In this sense the imagination takes on creative power and religious implications. It becomes a civilizing agency, one which frees man from those facts in his life which imprison his true nature and lead him to choose evil. The imagination has its most effective expression in language, in the use of words which provide the connecting link between the everyday world in which we must live, and the country of our desires. Words have power, and, finally, it is power with which Tolkien is concerned. He wishes to show how the imagination gives man power over his life, a life in which he may fight evil and defend good. A life in which the past, history, may be used to change the future and so affect the course of Time. A life in which, as Tolkien writes, man may realize "imagined wonder." This is the value to us of Tolkien's fiction: it suggests how we may use our imaginative power, our ability to "make" fantasy, paradoxically in order to know truth.

Such an intensely moral vision demands expression in a literary form which is not only firmly structured itself with well-defined purposes and ends, but which also makes use of traditional literary forms and themes: the romance and the novel, the theme of the mythic journey and the triumph of the hero over his people's enemies. Tolkien returns to these archetypal motifs because they still have emotional meaning for the modern reader and because they express the continuing power of the artist's imagination from age to age. *The Lord of the Rings* tells us, in both theme and structure, that we are not alone and that our world has meaning. And it tells us this through the power of a master "wordsmith," a writer who takes words, as a smith takes iron to the forge, and makes "things": in the case of *The Lord of the Rings*, a whole world which is consistent within itself and a universe analogous to our own, in which we may see ourselves. It is here that the wordsmith's power lies, in his creation of a double meaning, just as the word is both itself and also a meaning beyond itself. To see how this wordsmith operates, let us look first at Tolkien's statement about his art in a discussion of the fairy tale or "fantasy" before examining his major fictional creations, *The Hobbit,* and *The Lord of the Rings*. "On Fairy-stories" is an essay which provides the intellectual justification for the artist's "making of truth." It is here that the concept of realizing "imagined wonder" through words is explained.

Tolkien would find sympathetic support for his conception of the fairy tale or fantasy among writers of the past. William Blake, for example, thought of himself as a fantasy-maker. In "The Marriage of Heaven and Hell," Blake formulates his basic definition of the power of the imagination: "Everything possible to be believ'd is an image of truth." And again: "What is now proved was once only imagin'd." [2] Blake argues that all men are poets, and that they should trust their imaginations to guide them to the reality that lies behind the "facts" of the external world, a world our bodies and minds know as time and space, where clocks strike and deadlines must be kept, where the familiar feeling of leaves on trees or the wind in our hair suggests that our senses and the habits formed on the basis of what our senses tell us are guides to reality. For Blake this is a destructive submission to the "everyday" world. Man has reduced himself to a slave of his senses:

How do you know but ev'ry Bird that cuts the airy way,
Is an immense world of delight, clos'd by your senses five? [3]

That is, man knowing only what his eyes tell him, cannot

know the true world of the spirit. The bird seen flying in the air may be an angel to the imagination. If we can *imagine* that it is an angel, we have seen "an image of truth," "an immense world of delight" revealed beyond mere sensory perception. The imagination, in other words, is not just a faculty which dreams up unreal things in moments when we are tired or bored and look for escape from our routine lives. Blake conceives of it as a *power* man can willingly and joyfully exercise to experience "the world of delight." By imagining that world, man frees himself from his bondage to this one, which is not always delightful. To imagine, in other words, is to participate in the creation of the real world. This is to award man the possession of great power, and it is the meaning of this power which fantasists like Blake and Tolkien set out to explain in their imaginative writing. Both writers would agree that the mind is not merely a passive receiver of sense impressions, but an active instrument for creation, the realization of reality.

"Fantasy," Tolkien writes, is not only an equivalent term for what we call the "Imagination"; it also means "freedom from the domination of observed 'fact', in short of the fantastic." [4] Thus he sees the imagination's power to conceive of images of things which are not present in the world our senses know, as a virtue. The imagination works with images to achieve the desire which lies "at the heart of Faerie: the realization, independent of the conceiving mind, of imagined wonder." To make images of things is to make art, and so Tolkien takes pains to explain what art is, and how art is necessary in order to achieve the "desire" of which he writes. The art of the fantasist must be related to the everyday world in which he and his audience live, yet at the same time be part of that "other" world, the fantastic. This is where words become important because, for the storyteller, they are the bridge between the two. In stories they provide the images which express the work of the imagination, the "wonderful," to us. Further, their artful use by the storyteller convinces us of the reality of things which they describe. The imagination exercises its power over us through art, in the purposeful making of an imagined world through words. And we contribute to its power by reading the words and, as imagining beings, participating in the creation of the fantasy world.

Tolkien distinguishes between two worlds: the Primary and the Secondary. The Primary World concerns the spatial and temporal existence we know through our senses, through the routines of living. It is the world of nature and society, of families and teachers, bodies and babies, into which we are born and in which one day we will die, when our time runs out and the space we now occupy in this room on this street empties. It is the universe of observed fact in which we are imprisoned without our consent. But the power of the imagination enables man to enter a Secondary World created by the storyteller or wordsmith. This world is free of the Primary World, even though it must draw much of its imagery from events in time and space. By creating this other existence, the artist becomes a "sub-creator," a title designed to suggest the relationship of the artist to the Primary or "real" world. Like that world, his creation must seem consistent within itself, following observable laws and demanding, through its own proof, that we believe in it. Furthermore, such a world is implicit in the Primary World, and fulfills it, often provides it with meaning. This power to discover meaning through the imagination enables man to give form and value to nature and to transcend the "facts" of his existence.

> . . . natural objects can only be arrayed with a personal significance and glory by a gift, the gift of a person, of a man. Personality can only be derived from a person. The gods may derive their colour and beauty from the high splendours of nature, but it is Man who obtained these for them, abstracted them from sun and moon and cloud; their personality they get direct from him; the shadow or flicker of divinity that is upon them they receive through him from the invisible world, the Supernatural (p. 24).

The imagination brings the supernatural into the Primary World through its operation, and the "sub-creator" who tells a fairy story is therefore a pivotal figure, an integrator of the two worlds who does not reject one in order to enter the other. The act of sub-creation also serves to make man valuable in himself because he is there with his imagination to provide the connections; he is no longer to be seen as an outsider, an alien who is never to know "moral and emotional Truth," as Langbaum phrases it. Indeed, one of the great paradoxes of human existence for Tolkien is that the Primary World is necessary for the creation of the Secondary World. Every maker of a Secondary World hopes that in some way, the "peculiar quality of this secondary world (if not all the details) are derived from Reality, or are flowing into it" (p. 70). And Tolkien locates the sources for imagined reality in the feelings and wishes of human beings. He calls them "primal desires" that "lie near the heart of Faerie." Among these desires is the wish to "hold communion with other living things," that is, to talk with animals or trees. Another is the desire to live forever. These wishes are human and arise from man's life in the Primary World. And in this world man's wishes operate: an "essential power of Faerie," Tolkien tells us, is to make the visions of fantasy "immediately effective by the will." In this manner "natural objects" obtain their meaning, their "significance and glory" as a "gift" from man. Such opportunity may seem unimaginable to us if we are accustomed to see only "partial meanings" in experience, and to feel that effort in a meaningless universe is vain. But to say that man wishes to make his visions "effective" is to argue that he is active and constructive, that he has a will, and that he can shape his life according to his vision of the great truths which, Tolkien believes, exist for us. The invisible world, the Supernatural, is manifest through man, and in this view, he regains his significance in the world which much contemporary thought and writing seem to deny him.

If we can turn back, now, to the place of the artist between the Primary and Secondary Worlds, we can see how he serves to make "imagined wonder" real to us. The fantasy or fairy-story is the form, according to Tolkien, in which the artist works best. The "sub-creator" must work with words, and it is through words that the connection between worlds is made. Tolkien tells us that it "was in fairy-stories that I first divined the potency of the words, and the wonder of the things, such as stone, and wood, and iron; tree and grass; house and fire; bread and wine." And it was perhaps in this early reading of fairy stories that the author of *The Lord of the Rings* got his start as a wordsmith who wished to exercise the power words and images possess, the power to reveal the "wonder" hidden in things. Tolkien, we should remember, is a philologist, a student of language and of ancient texts often written in tongues no longer spoken. He says elsewhere that he began the Trilogy with "primarily linguistic" inspiration, "to provide the necessary background of 'history' for Elvish tongues [the languages of the elves]" which he had been inventing.[5] History is to a large extent the account of how power has been exercised in the past. It may in turn forecast how it will be used in the future. So Tolkien wished to provide an historic world in which the wonder expressed in elvish words and songs could be placed.

This may sound either whimsical or pedantic on the author's part, but it is neither. This "rationale" for *The Lord of the Rings* argues instead for its author's respect for the word as a beautiful and powerful instrument for "realizing wonder." It also suggests his interest in the realities of power exercised in the Primary World, not only in some dream realm divorced from human problems. "Language," he writes in "On Fairy-Stories," cannot "be dismissed. The incarnate mind, the tongue, and the tale are in our world coeval." Our tongue gives form to our imaginings; it gives man the *power* to form a "story" which not only takes on a life of its own but is also Blake's "image of truth" man's tongue makes. This identification of man and his creation means, too, that man reveals himself through his "art," and is particularly himself when he uses words.

Hence Tolkien's praise, for that everyday element of human speech, the lowly adjective.

29

The human mind, endowed with the powers of generalization and abstraction, sees not only *green-grass*, discriminating it from other things (and finding it fair to look upon), but sees that it is *green* as well as being *grass*. But how powerful, how stimulating to the very faculty that produced it, was the invention of the adjective: no spell or incantation in Faerie is more potent (p. 22).

The making of an adjective is a power given to man which enables him to reveal meaning in the world he describes. And by awakening his descriptive ability, an adjective makes man a partner in that world. Grass is not only grass; it is green, soft, beautiful and growing— among other things. Man gives of himself to make grass interesting, noting its beauty or utility, placing it in the total context of a world. To describe something in Nature with words is to give Nature value and to make Man the Namer—not a passive observer of "facts," but a creator of reality.

The mind that thought of *light, heavy, grey, yellow, still, swift* also conceived of magic that would make heavy things light and able to fly, turn grey lead into yellow gold, and the still rock into a swift water. If it could do the one, it could do the other; it inevitably did both. When we take green from grass, blue from heaven, and red from blood, we have already an enchanter's power—upon one plane; and the desire to wield that power in the world external to our minds awakes. . . . But in such "fantasy," as it is called, new form is made; Faerie begins; Man becomes a sub-creator (p. 22).

The task of the "sub-creator" is to make the reader of his fantasy believe fully in the Secondary World which he creates, and so his use of words must be both evocative and convincing. And since words have their source, as fantasy does, in the "primal desires" of man, they must

30

be used carefully so that no one is harmed. We can see the close connections between words and basic human desires in stories of magic and magical incantations where, if the right words are spoken in the right way, reality will be revealed according to the speaker's wish. Ali Baba opens the hidden treasure-cave by saying, "Open Sesame." At a moment of intense fear, when Frodo and Sam are being attacked by the giant spider, Shelob, Sam, with the glass of Galadriel in his hand, cries aloud "in a language which he did not know":

> A Elbereth Gilthoniel
> o menel palan-díriel,
> le nallon sí di'nguruthos!
> A tíro nin, Fanuilos!

And these words put him in contact with the elemental forces in the world that are fighting against such evils as Shelob. With this call to the powers of goodness in the universe, Sam's "indomitable spirit" recovers its potency, and "with that he staggered to his feet and was Samwise the hobbit, . . . again." Words give their user power over the natural world. They put him in contact with the supernatural which reveals itself from within things. They give him a sense of his worth, his own "indomitable spirit," and so he becomes, once again, a power for good. The language Sam speaks here is elvish, and here he shares in the life, however distant, of those enlightened beings, the elves, realizing another of the "primal desires" Tolkien credits to our account: "to hold communion with other living things." In Sam's words, we find an example of the way in which created beings "exercise power in the world external" to their minds. Their power carries Sam to his feet, and he raises his sword against the terrible spider.

The making of words, then, their "saying," provides an analogy for the way in which the imagination operates. Furthermore, they give man power over Nature because they express reality, the inner meaning of things and events. In this sense, the creation of fantasy, the world of Faerie, is not a flight from reality, an escape from the

31

responsibility which power demands. It is an act which serves certain positive purposes in the Primary World. By making words, the sub-creator is in touch with the basic truths of life, and therefore presents us with a vision which is liberating at the same time that it explains and inspires.

Fantasy does not mean a dream world without roots in human reality, nor does "fairy story" mean a light tale involving small human figures with wings. Instead, Tolkien thinks of the Fairy-story or Fantasy as a high form of art, "the operative link between Imagination and the final result, Sub-creation." In fantasy, man finds equivalents for his primal desires and for his visions of reality in created beings, the images of his imagination. In this way fantasy is an equivalent of imagination in its suggestion of "freedom from the domination of observed 'fact', in short of the fantastic."

> I am thus not only aware but glad of the etymological and semantic connexions of *fantasy* with *fantastic*: with images of things that are not only "not actually present," but which are indeed not to be found in our primary world at all, or are generally believed not to be found there (p. 47).

And this "freedom from observed fact" is a positive value, "a virtue not a vice." This is because the exercise of the imagination is a healthy activity in which man recognizes his freedom from the routine, the spiritually destructive affairs of his life in the Primary World; and in making fantasy, man gives form to otherwise unrealizable desires.

One of these is simply "the making or glimpsing of Other-worlds." Tolkien here suggests that all men may be sub-creators, for to "make" a vision of some other way of life than our own is to "glimpse" or "see" it. The terms are interchangeable. Another desire is to communicate with other created beings. Men with any sensitivity to the life in nature—the motions of trees, the near-language of streams among the rocks, the quiet, thoughtless presence of cows in a pasture—have surely supposed that each of these things spoke a language which men could learn. In fairy-stories, of course, birds and horses do speak. (In "Cinderella" a bird gives the despised heroine gold and silver dresses to wear to the Prince's ball, and later warns the Prince that the stepsisters are false. In "The Goose Girl" the head of a horse advises the heroine how to win her love.)

Yet another desire is to achieve immortality. The fear of death can be expressed and resolved by its manifestation in sleep, or in living to be very old. The Sleeping Beauty is finally awakened by a kiss from her Prince; fairy godmothers, good kings and queens (and evil ones), and lovers seem to live forever. Tolkien's wish as a child was to meet a dragon: "I desired dragons with a profound desire." He satisfied this desire by creating Smaug, in *The Hobbit*, a formidable beast who could trace his fantasy ancestry back to the firedrake Beowulf fights in another "fairy-story." An "essential power of Faerie," Tolkien tells us, as though he were providing a comment on his own creation, is to make the visions of fantasy "immediately effective by the will." The young child's wish was realized in the mature author who exercised his imagination and his freedom from fact through a purposive creative act. He imagined wonder.

So, in one sense, fantasy is the fulfillment of man's wishes, but in place of relegating such visions to the irrational and irrelevant, Tolkien argues that man fulfills himself by this act of "sub-creation." One could say that, after all, we are superstitious and emotional creatures first, and only rational last. Buried deep in our bones is the need to have faith in a meaningful world not always available to the rational mind. Wishes, primal desires, dreams, are part of man's world, and thus honorable, valuable, not to be denied. Furthermore, Tolkien consistently associates these visions founded upon human aspirations with "images of truth," with eternal realities that find expression in talking birds and horses and awakened princesses. This Secondary World is Blake's "immense world of delight" that lies beyond the objects of sensory perception. In this sense, nothing is "made-up";

rather, the ideal nature of man is given reality. Man can be perfected through his art, insofar as perfection means the discovery of truth. For, as we shall see, Tolkien believes in an ordered and morally meaningful universe which man's fantasies "make effective."

In summary, we can say that fantasy or fairy-story, as Tolkien uses the term, is a creation of the imagination which uses words to evoke reality. Thus the words used in magic spells not only open hidden treasures in the earth, or unlock the secret stairs into the depths of Moria; words cast in the form of a fairy-story give form to the acts of the imagination, and so magic spells and the elvish languages are analogies for the power of the mind. For behind Tolkien's interest in words as the basis for history is his sense that the outer world we know with our senses hides or disguises an "inner" world which is not chaotic, meaningless, destructively materialistic in its effects, but instead is ordered, meaningful, spiritually elevating; words can be seen as part of the fabric disguising reality, but, better, they are the means of depicting reality, letting it out, paradoxically, as they weave the tapestry of the fairy-story. The premise of fantasy is that life is single and purposeful, and that "what is hidden shall be revealed." This is the task of the metaphor, the image with a meaning hidden and yet more than it is, and which is both the door and the key in the door. Words hide in order to reveal: the true prince appears only after his beloved has passed through many trials and proved her worthiness by much suffering. When the young princes are turned into swans by a wicked stepmother, their sister sews silently, never to speak a word, for six years until she has made six shirts from the petals of the star-flower to throw over them and return them to mortal life. After many trials, she succeeds and the swans are revealed to be men (although one is left with a wing in place of an arm because his sister could not quite finish his magic shirt). In such fairy-stories it is not reason which exposes truth, or brings wishes to fruition (the same thing). It is the imagination which saves the day. It is for this reason that Tolkien can write that "Fantasy can thus be explained as a sudden glimpse of the underlying reality or truth." It is for this reason, too, that he can describe the fantasy world as a moral one, because it exposes and confirms ultimate, universal truth.

Indeed, one explanation for the appeal to many readers of *The Lord of the Rings* or any other fantasy is that it is essentially a religious experience to read such works. Faith in the imagined world is vital to fantasy, and to us. For it cannot exist if we do not believe in it, and if we cannot have faith in a meaningful world, then we must live in alienation and despair. Put another way, the task of the sub-creator is to create a world in which we can believe through his art. He must make a consistent, wonderful vision in which all that takes place there is "true," and we must be able to accept his vision as genuine. This gift which we as readers make to the artist if he paints or writes well is what Tolkien calls "Secondary Belief." The great fantasies are those in which the enchanter's art most successfully serves its purpose.

Actually, this emphasis upon the power of words to give us a glimpse of the "underlying reality or truth" serves several important moral ends. Only one of these ends is the evocation of faith in the wonder of the well-told fantasy. Tolkien goes further and makes explicit how *healthy* such faith can be through its effect in the Primary World. In "On Fairy-Stories" Tolkien provides an explanation for the impression a perfectly conceived imaginative work has on us through the power we permit it to exercise. We remember a poem, a painting, a musical composition because, when we first experienced them, they changed our way of perceiving the world and our feelings about life. The imaginative experience modifies our sense of reality; it satisfies not only our aesthetic sense but some deeper element in us as well. That element is religious in nature.

A contemporary critic, Northrop Frye, writes that the imagination presents us with a vision which frees us. The world of the imagination is that of a "power, which contains morality, beauty, and truth but is never subordinated to them," and "rises free of all their compulsions." That is, the imagination gives form to these ideals, and contains all of them, and then gives us something more.

The work of imagination presents us with a vision, not of the personal greatness of the poet, but of something impersonal and far greater: the vision of a decisive act of spiritual freedom, the vision of the recreation of man.[6]

The imagination thus performs the greatest spiritual act, a "vision" of perfected man which promises him release from the Primary World and from our limited concept of ourselves. Frye is not willing to argue that the imagination actually *works* to effect change in this world; he would be unwilling to say that this freedom is an instance of faith turned into knowledge, of a vision made "real." Tolkien, however, goes further than Frye in arguing that this vision can be realized and that moral acts are dictated by what the imagination knows to be true. Tolkien would agree with Frye that the vision of "underlying reality or truth" is not designed to advance the personal greatness of the poet. However, it reveals through him the greater world Tolkien calls "Joy."

In the first place, the realization of "imagined wonder" invites us to free ourselves from the Primary World through vision. We can become too accustomed to life; we tend to take for granted leaves on the trees, the color of the sky, the face of someone we love, worst of all, ourselves, prisoners in the world of habit which dulls and petrifies. With "creative fantasy" we can achieve what Tolkien calls "recovery":

Recovery (which includes return and renewal of health) is a re-gaining—regaining of a clear view. . . . We need, in any case, to clean our windows; so that the things seen clearly may be freed from the drab blur of triteness or familiarity—from possessiveness (p. 57).

Possessiveness is destructive of values because we do not then permit things, other beings, to have a life of their own. We become habituated to our vision of other lives—from insects on a leaf to human beings in our home—and

36

we ignore the ultimate beauty in their difference from us. For to know is to possess, and this can be dangerous if we do not exercise this power over them with respect.

> . . . the things that are trite, or (in a bad sense) familiar, are the things that we have appropriated, legally or mentally. We say we know them. They have become like the things which once attracted us by their glitter, or their colour, or their shape, and we laid hands on them, and then locked them in our hoard, acquired them, and acquiring ceased to look at them (p. 58).

Such possession is destructive of the ever-changing life of such things. It also makes our view of ourselves "trite," locking us into an egocentric self-vision equally unchangeable because we seem to find such a condition reflected in the world around us. Tolkien illustrates this condition in his description of Sauron, who wishes to possess the world by capturing the minds of living beings and turning them into slaves or machines; in Tolkien, one becomes enslaved through the denial of his imaginative life. Orcs are frightening creatures because they have no imaginations and, in consequence, no sense of the beauty of other living things. The two things go together, and Sauron must stamp them out if he is to rule a world made over in his image.

> Creative fantasy, because it is mainly trying to do something else (make something new), may open your hoard and let all the locked things fly away like cage-birds. The gems all turn into flowers or flames, and you will be warned that all you had (or knew) was dangerous and potent, not really effectively chained, free and wild; no more yours than they were you (pp. 58–9).

By seeing things newly, by putting the familiar objects from the Primary World into unfamiliar stories and

37

exotic contexts, we can re-experience the world outside ourselves, and with that sense of wonder which occurs when we find the world different from our expectations. In fantasy the life of the imagination and the life of the everyday world touch and illuminate each other. And in the wonder we feel at a discovered but hidden life, we have, in little, a vision of our own "recreation." As in fairy-stories, in Tolkien's fantasies we find the unexpected in the expected: hobbits on their journeys encounter talking trees, for instance, altering their preconceived notions about trees. Yet the ents sleep, bathe, fall in love, and join in the battle against Sauron because they, too, participate in a "real" world. The hobbits' experience with the ents provides an analogy, in turn, for our response to hobbits; because we have never met any creatures like them before, we wonder at them and at the imaginative power of the mind that introduced them to us. But we also see something of our familiar world in that of the hobbits, who are as prone to greed, courage and fear as we are, and who therefore extend our awareness of imagined creatures whose existence is different than ours without becoming improbable and, so, unbelievable.

Creative fantasy operates not only to free us from possessiveness; it has a statement to make about the real nature of the world. "Underlying reality or truth" is hidden from us in the Primary World, but with the imagination we can perceive ultimate reality, and actually bring it into our own experience; we can realize "imagined wonder" as something "independent of the conceiving mind," as ultimate truth. So when we fantasize, when we wish for something, such as an escape from death, or to speak to other living things, or to fly like a bird, we are not simply escaping from a painful life in the Primary World. We are seeking fulfillment of our spiritual knowledge in an affirmation of what we know to be a meaningful universe. In "On Fairy-Stories," Tolkien writes that fantasy provides not only healthy "recovery" from possessiveness. It also provides escape and consolation. Escape is not to flee from the world, but to affirm its value by seeking to realize wishes and desires. The great wish is to have a "happy ending" to a story. In a "fairy-story" like "Cinderella" we suffer with the oppressed girl forced by cruel stepdaughters and a stepmother to slave in the kitchen. We go with the disguised Cinderella to the Prince's ball, hoping she will be home by midnight, hoping the Prince will find her and rescue her from her kitchen. When, at last, Cinderella is called in to try on the glass slipper our wish that she be recognized for what she is, really a princess, is fulfilled. Right triumphs, the unjust are punished, and order and purpose are again affirmed in the world.

In part we have observed the power of words to create a Secondary World which, in one sense, is a disguised world, one in which truth is hidden so that it must be searched for. We know that Cinderella has the beauty, the virtue, and the destiny to marry a prince; her story creates in us a sense of wonder at the happy ending not because it surprises us but because it fulfills our hopes. Like us, Cinderella is "disguised" in order that her true nature and fate be revealed. Creative fantasy thus provides an analogy with the Primary World where we must search constantly for the meaning of an event, for the final truth in a person or an experience, and in its discovery recognize values. We acknowledge the value of suffering which disguise imposes on us, but we know it for what it is: Cinderella must be disguised in order to be revealed. The Happy Ending is not a flight from reality, but a revelation of it.

Here, too, we have the source for the epic journey, the Quest, which Bilbo makes in his journey to the East, which Frodo makes with the Ring on the long and painful attempt to throw it back into the Cracks of Doom. Bilbo seeks to find a treasure; Frodo to destroy one. Both, however, seek ultimate truth which is revealed only with suffering and trial. But it is the final act which is important because such fantasy provides us with an analogy for our own journey which should have a Happy Ending, too. Bilbo in *The Hobbit* does help recover the treasure for the dwarves, and is instrumental in righting wrong. Frodo succeeds in throwing the Ring into the Cracks of Doom, bringing down the great enemy, Sauron, and so initiating the new age of Man. By analogy, men may also change the world, make events happen, reveal truth. Rather than an irresponsible escape from suffering, the Happy Ending is an affirmation of our power to know "Joy." Joy does not deny sorrow and failure in the world, but it does deny "universal final defeat"; it offers us "grace," the divine gift of mercy, affirmation of the triumph of good, of order and meaning.

In other words, fantasy as an imaginative creation is always an account of our own lives. Its end, like its contents, expresses man's power because it expresses God's power. The wonder we feel at a Happy Ending is the manifestation of our delight in our freedom from observed fact and our discovery, necessarily to be repeated over and over, of our own recreation. But Tolkien suggests that the vision of this truth is more than a wish: it is an act of freedom in itself which repeats in each man the truth of his own nature: not imprisoned and in despair, but immortal and joyous. Joy, for Tolkien, has finally a Christian character, for it is deliverance of the soul, that Joy known when the soul is reunited with God. Fantasy provides us with heroes like Frodo and heroines like Cinderella who achieve redemption, and therefore can promise this final joy to us. Tolkien's use of terms like "grace" and "deliverance" should suggest that for him fantasy is allegorical, taking its ultimate meaning from what he calls "the Christian Story." The truth "glimpsed" in a fairy-story is heavenly, that Joy which the Christian soul seeks to know as a Happy End. The "joy of deliverance" is an affirmation of God's world which appears in our world as the fairy-story Happy Ending.

Tolkien makes this religious undersupport for fantasy explicit in his reading of the "Christian Story," as he calls it, as a "fairy-story." "Eucatastrophe" is his term for the "reversal" of tragic action.

> The Gospels contain a fairy-story, or a story of a larger kind which embraces all the essence of fairy-stories. They contain many marvels—peculiarly artistic, beautiful, and moving; "mythical" in their perfect, self-contained significance;

and among the marvels is the greatest and most complete conceivable eucatastrophe (p. 71).

That is, the birth of Christ and his Resurrection after death are fantastic: they express the fulfillment of man's wishes; they are realizations of "imagined wonder"; Christ's "story begins and ends in joy. It has pre-eminently the 'inner consistency of reality.'" But Tolkien is really suggesting that this ultimate "fiction" is the prototype for all sub-creation, and the joy of the Christian Resurrection is the basis for our feeling of "wonder" in every Happy Ending. Christ's dual nature as god and man is the analogy for all story-telling, for all reality which is real and unreal, spirit and matter, the "bird" that is also an angel though not perceived as such by our "senses five," in Blake's lines. Every story of adventures by a journeying hero, every account of the trials of Cinderella, has a hidden meaning which in its discovery, reveals God's intent. The work of the imagination is, by definition, revelatory and symbolic. The Christian God works in this manner.

. . . God redeemed the corrupt making-creatures, men, in a way fitting to this aspect, as to others of their strange nature (p. 71).

Where Truth is infinite, Man, "for whom this was done," is finite, and so he must use the means of knowing Truth fitted to his condition. Thus the fairy-story is a version of the greatest story, that of man's redemption, a version which he can read and understand: "It looks forward . . . to the Great Eucatastrophe. . . . this story is supreme; and it is true." Such a basis for evaluating imaginative experience rests upon a deeply Christian faith on Tolkien's part. It also affirms the purposive interaction of every element, fictional and real, of God's world, elements to be read as corresponding to each other: God's creatures reveal him, just as the life of Christ reveals God on the one hand, and the purpose and course of man's life, on the other.

Tolkien denies that he has written an allegory—that is,

41

a fictional story with specific moral meaning connected to each character and event. But the general lines of allegory are everywhere evident in *The Lord of the Rings,* and a Christian reading of fantasy and man's history must ultimately be moral and hence allegorical. The fairy-story or fantasy is almost always based upon a struggle between good and evil. It tells of the recovery of man to spiritual health, in depicting a Happy Ending which prefigures the promised redemptive Happy Ending, the triumph of good over evil, of Christian theology. Tolkien is very clear that by his imaginative creation man realizes this larger Joy in the Primary World.

> The Christian has still to work, with mind
> as well as body, to suffer, hope, and die; but he
> may now perceive that all his bents and faculties
> have a purpose, which can be redeemed. . . . in
> Fantasy he may actually assist in the effoliation
> and multiple enrichment of creation (p. 73).

Furthermore, we will find in *The Lord of the Rings* that the contemporary problems of the world are treated in the history of Frodo's world, and that incidents in his journey to Mordor duplicate or echo incidents in the life of Christ. We cannot forget that fairy-stories reaffirm for us the triumph of good over evil, and therefore the existence of an ordered universe behind the seeming disorder in the Primary World. But allegory need not be the dry account of abstractions like Justice or Peace which are only intellectual in their effect. Allegory is everywhere about us in the Primary World, and can appear in the struggles of men or of hobbits to bring about the world's redemption. Because all creatures are part of God's planned universe, their lives will always be symbolic of that world's misery and joy, its beginning and end. But Tolkien is not only Christian in his reading of Primary and Secondary Worlds; he studies the past (the history of the hobbits or of the ages of Middle-earth prior to the Age of Man, for instance), in order to reveal its moral meaning. Here Tolkien is like the Renaissance Christian (for example, Edmund Spenser, in his allegorical poem *The*

Fairy Queen): history and morality reveal the same truth. For Tolkien, history is both an account of the sources of our present life, and an *analogy* for our present life: the struggle between good and evil, and the recovery of man. History is the study of power and how it has been used for destructive or beneficent ends.

Put another way, we can say that Tolkien is writing myth, not only in the sense of an imagined story, but in the sense of something larger. Myth also refers to a story of cosmic importance in which heroes defy the gods or perhaps, act like gods; in any event myth suggests the presentation of the supernatural in our own world. Myths of gods and heroes give us images of archetypal human experience which have an imaginative and emotional effect upon us, and so convince us of their ultimate Truth. The most universal of these myths is that of the hero who sets off to gain knowledge for his people on a Quest. Often this involves a journey into Hell, the underworld, or into the dangerous wildwood beyond civilization. There he encounters strange or supernatural beings, must often fight for his life, or suffer torment before escape or release; but always his spiritual qualities are tested as well as his physical strength. In the end he returns, having conquered the dragon, been transfigured into a higher being, or carrying the Golden Bough, the Green Girdle, the sign of his secret penetration to the ultimate mysteries of the universe. We can see that much of this description covers the life of Christ, on the one hand, and the life of Frodo, on the other. We will return to the particular details of this myth as Tolkien develops them in his fantasies, but the point here is that myth in its appeal, whether to primitive or sophisticated audiences, demands a religious response: we must *believe* in the quester and his search; we must have faith that he will succeed. Our emotional response to mythic journeys suggests that we can realize our own particular vision through such images. Thus myth or fantasy satisfies man's need to find more in life than that which he sees before him in the Primary World. Myth relates man to his world, rather than perpetuating that alienation from it which is often described as the curse of modern life.

43

In its mythic content—the journey of a hero (or heroes) through strange adventures and his return, having saved his people from destruction by evil forces—*The Lord of the Rings* is the story of the soul's journey toward salvation or the learned man's search for wisdom; the attempt to defeat chaos through willed, individual effort and to announce the perfectability of man through images, words, fantasy. Such a vision is apocalyptic in its meaning; at the end of the journey, truth will be revealed in a perfected heaven and earth, and man will have become what he was meant to be: the imagination itself, as Blake would say. Tolkien's faith in the human animal to perfect himself and thus to illustrate the purposive nature of the cosmos demands a religious response from his readers.

We can say that Tolkien's interest in the power of words lies in his use of them to achieve the triumph of truth and the perfection of the sub-creator, the maker of words himself. To use words is to assume power over the worlds they depict; to ascribe meaning to an event or to make a mythic story for an imagined hero is to reveal the true meaning of life, and so to "realize" imagined wonder in the Primary World. Hence the importance to Tolkien of the Sub-Creative Art: that of the storyteller, whose task is also religious in nature. The writer must make his readers *believe* in the Secondary World he creates for them:

> What really happens is that the story-maker proves a successful "sub-creator." He makes a Secondary World which your mind can enter. Inside it, what he relates is "true": it accords with the laws of that world. You therefore believe it, while you are, as it were, inside. The moment disbelief arises, the spell is broken: the magic, or rather art, has failed (p. 37).

Thus the writer of fantasy must write about universal, mythic human experience; the conflict between good and evil must provide the moral basis for the structure of his "history." But he must also carve a beautiful Secondary World from the rough rock of experience, an artful act

44

which like the magician's emphasizes the primacy of the imagination and its revelation of truth over the Primary World. He must give us details from our own life which help us to accept his description of a fantastic creature like a hobbit or a dragon. The sub-creator bridges both worlds, for the qualities of this secondary world "are derived from Reality, or are flowing into it." And this flow, hopefully, will bring the two worlds together, and at the same time, integrate the sub-creator, the artist, in his creation. He will not be merely the plaything of Nature, the victim of every disease of the body, every passion of the heart. He will become civilized, and a civilizing agent who reveals imagined wonder and therefore, truth and order. It is no wonder that Tolkien pays particular attention in *The Lord of the Rings* not to Gandalf the Magician so much as to Gandalf the Artist whose knowledge of history and the languages of the past enables him to shape time and space to his own purposes, and who is changed himself from Gandalf the Gray to Gandalf the White in the course of his Quest to save civilization. The power to realize an imaginative vision gives man control over the Primary World, but he must exercise his power with discretion, and with love. For power can destroy the possessor if he uses it only for selfish ends, and by "destroy" Tolkien means "de-civilize," to become like an animal.

And perhaps this is a crucial distinction to make between the poets of creative fantasy like William Blake and the sub-creator, Tolkien. Blake sees man "cleansing his perceptions" in order to perceive the bird that is really an angel. One must become a visionary like Blake himself, and leave the things of this earth for heavenly things. The images we have of the great figures of Biblical history—Noah, Jonah, Jesus himself—are spiritual entities. And Blake describes how the imagination might be able to take man into the true or spiritual world with them:

> If the Spectator could Enter into these Images
> in his Imagination, approaching them on the
> Fiery Chariot of his Contemplative Thought,

> if he could Enter into Noah's Rainbow or into
> his bosom, or could make a Friend & Com-
> panion of one of these Images of wonder, which
> always intreats him to leave mortal things (as
> he must know), then would he arise from his
> Grave, then would he meet the Lord in the
> Air & then he would be happy.'

This is a visionary poet's version of the Apocalypse, when
perfected Man will realize himself and there will no
longer be any need for words because the gap between the
mind and the body, the soul and the physical world, will
be bridged, closed up, through man's abandonment of
"mortal things." Blake is asking man to actually "enter
into these images," riding in "the Fiery Chariot of his
Contemplative Thought," and thus to lift himself into
freedom through the mind's imaginative power. A man
becomes an "image of truth" himself in that he partici-
pates through the power of the imagination in God's
Truth.

But Blake is asking for a transformation through vision
of which most men are not capable. Tolkien is less
ambitious—and rather more realistic. Unlike Blake, he
does not wish to abandon the Primary World, but, instead, to express its spiritual meaning in a manner con-
genial to the finite nature of man. Tolkien is not a mystic
or a visionary, although he may make use of visionary
experience in presenting the religious theme in the life
of Frodo or Gandalf. As an historian, Tolkien is interested
in the way the imagination has worked in the past in the
Primary World, and in discovering the connections with
the present. History provides him with a living world in
which hobbits and men, elves and orcs function as living
men might function in the Primary World. The sub-creator's task is to make us believe in the Secondary World
thus created, not in order to "throw off" the real world,
but in order to live in it for good and not evil. Fantasy
permits us to glimpse other worlds, and to participate
in their creation as readers in the temporal, phenomenal
world we now inhabit. As a student of the history of
words, the sub-creator knows that words have power,

and that power must be used for good. Man must constantly choose between good and evil, and in his choices man expresses the teachings of religion which help him in the battle against evil. The sub-creator must make us believe in that battle. He must provide us with an analogy for our lives in the imagined lives of other created beings, and, by showing us some final Joy through his story, express the greatest Joy we will find at the end of our journey in this world. The imaginative vision must be realized on earth, and we must show how Tolkien uses his power as a wordsmith to make this happen.

We must make a circle back to the beginnings of Tolkien's art in order to explain the shape of his ideas and how his imagination gave life to the mythic and literary traditions which he used in his creation, giving them new life for modern readers. We have seen that his creative fantasy has its start in his own wishes, but he is careful to rely upon traditional fictional forms in which to tell his story. For we must be made to believe in this Secondary World of hobbits and orcs, and Tolkien borrows his colors and patterns, not only from the Primary World we know, but also from the fantasy world of fairy-story we also know from centuries of storytelling. Like the One Ring our imaginative history circles back into the past, and forward into the future as well. This means that Tolkien can write about elves and hobbits, for instance, as created beings living in an earlier age than ours, and yet say something about the Age of Man in which we live. Created beings have similar lives, overlapping concerns, because they must all deal with good and evil and the problem of power and its effects upon the world. Power is a perennial element in our lives, and the structure of words we have erected over the centuries to control and guide it has become a power for good or evil, too. Hence the value of examining the forms these words have taken historically, to see how Tolkien has employed his imagination and the traditional forms he has used in shaping his Secondary World. We can also say that like the One Ring of the Trilogy, such an historical inheritance presents a challenge to the present, throwing into question old values exactly as it offers a threat to the new generation that must deal with it.

In order to see how Tolkien worked to write a history which would satisfy the standards set in "On Fairy-Stories" and at the same time provide us with a symbolic history of our own time, we should look first at the forms the imagination takes in his work. This is the "art" which will sustain our belief in the Secondary World or let it fall. And following Tolkien's turn to the past, we must look, too, at the basic structural element in both *The Hobbit* and *The Lord of the Rings* to see how Tolkien has used forms and themes which he has borrowed from the past. This basic element is the Quest, the circular journey which the heroes make in both books. We want to know what the value of this mythic or archetypal journey is, and we want to know something about the fantasy world of the Romance with its medieval settings in which Tolkien seems to have located the hobbits' adventures. We will then examine the types of creatures described by Tolkien and note the precedents for their lives in our own history. Finally, we should be able to say something about the ultimate meanings of Tolkien's world, and why it appeals so strongly today to the modern reader.

Perhaps it would be helpful to return to the suggestion that the One Ring of *The Lord of the Rings* provides an illuminating metaphor both for the structure of Tolkien's work and any analysis of it. In *The Hobbit* and *The Lord of the Rings* the One Ring influences the lives of its possessors. In both books, a hobbit sets out on a Quest which takes him away from his familiar countryside and into strange, often desperate adventures. In *The Hobbit,* Bilbo finds the Ring, claims it from the creature which had lost it, the Gollum, and uses the Ring's power to grant invisibility to accomplish the Quest's goal: in this case, to recover the dwarves' treasure under the Lonely Mountain from the dragon, Smaug. In *The Lord of the Rings,* the Quest's goal is reversed, and its meaning extended to comment far more significantly upon the moral and spiritual nature of Middle-earth. In the Trilogy,

Frodo's task is not to recover a treasure at the end of the Quest, but to destroy one: the One Ring of Power which will guarantee the triumph of evil and the loss of freedom should it be recovered by its Maker, Sauron. With the help of many other creatures, Frodo succeeds in destroying the Ring in the Cracks of Doom; his Quest completed, Frodo finally departs from Middle-earth, along with the other creatures, such as elves and Gandalf the Magician, who have completed their historic tasks and leave the world to the new Age of Men, which they have helped to bring about.

The Ring thus symbolizes the cyclic character of the Quest, the return of the questors to their beginning. But it also symbolizes the recurrent character of history. For in the previous Age Sauron had also attempted to overthrow civilization, and been defeated. The evil which he represented lived on, as did he, and in the Ring he succeeded in perpetuating his power so that the journeys and wars recorded in *The Lord of the Rings* were undertaken to finally achieve his overthrow. After Bilbo has passed the Ring on to his nephew, Frodo, and left him with the problem it represents, Gandalf explains to the puzzled and frightened hobbit the meaning of the One Ring. Originally there were a number of rings made by the master artisans, the elves, twenty in all. They were magic and powerful rings. Three were kept for the "Elven-kings under the sky." Seven went to the "Dwarf-lords in their halls of stone." Nine of the rings were given to "Mortal Men doomed to die." And the One Ring which, we are told, was "to rule them all" was kept by Sauron himself, the Dark Lord. In a great battle years before *The Lord of the Rings*, Sauron was defeated and the Ring cut from his hand by a champion of men, Isildur, who in turn lost it dying in battle. The Ring fell into the great river, Anduin, and was there found by the Gollum and in turn by Bilbo the Hobbit who brought it up once again into the light of Middle-earth. This is the "Shadow of the Past," that is, history, with which created beings must deal in *The Lord of the Rings*.

Tolkien turns this small bit of gold into a symbol for Sauron's power and potential for evil in created beings like

Men. But it is also a power itself, a power for evil, for it was made by Sauron, who put a great deal of his own power into it, "so that he could rule all the others." If he can recover this One Ring, Sauron will then control the rest, and the possessors of the other rings.

The Magic Ring, the controlling symbol for Tolkien's fantasy, has a long history in our folklore. Usually it has come out of some hidden hoard, and is associated with the secrets of the earth, chthonic powers of Nature which are buried in the dark, until evoked by worshippers of the darker forces of life. The ring of the Nibelungen is just such a treasure, and its possessor seeks to control frightening, mysterious forces usually beyond man's, even the gods', control. In this sense the One Ring symbolizes the chaotic world beyond order and civilization which strives continually to break into the upper world of men and overthrow what structures the imagination has erected there. In another equally traditional sense, the One Ring is the Life Force itself which has the potential for evil or for good: Sauron, Gandalf tells Frodo, was not evil originally, but was perverted like the great prototype of evil beings, the fallen angel, Satan. Thus the Ring can symbolize the potential for evil or for good in all created beings.

And we can follow the working out of this threat to order and value in such creatures as the Ringwraiths, the Mortal Men given nine of the original rings who were brought to destruction by such ownership; they pass from being men to becoming slaves of the Dark Lord, frightening shadows swooping about the dark roads and skies of Middle-earth on Sauron's evil errands. Tolkien has carefully followed in the paths of his great storytelling predecessors and given the One Ring the ambiguous value of all such buried treasure. Gold is often an end in itself; if the peasant's daughter can spin straw into gold overnight, she will marry the king—and with the help of the "little man" or gnome, a figure traditionally associated with buried hoards of gold, she succeeds. But, in securing Rumpelstiltskin's aid, she almost loses her first child to him; evil nearly triumphs. And the One Ring, too, is desirable for its power. But it can destroy its owner. For like great wealth or great power, the One Ring is a challenge: it gives power according to the ability, the strength, and the spirit of its possessor. Those who live in the world of imaginative truth, like Gandalf and Galadriel, the ruler of the elves remaining in Middle-earth, do not seek to own this dangerous treasure; they recognize that not even they can control it for long. Gollum becomes progressively possessed by the Ring; he was always weak, without will and spirit, and so became its victim quickly, once he emerged in pursuit of it into the upper world. The Ring has the power to confer invisibility upon its wearer; Bilbo, accidentally slipping it on in Gollum's cave, continues to use it to avoid nasty encounters with his relatives when he has returned to the Shire. And even though he is careful to use it only rarely, he begins to feel its effect, which makes him increasingly shadow-like, "thin and stretched," a sign, says Gandalf, "that the ring was getting control." Bilbo begins to lose that most precious of things, his own nature, to an external force. Here, Tolkien reminds us of the ring of Gyges, described by Plato, which conferred invisibility upon a young man who, in love with the queen, murdered her husband and took the widow and the crown for himself. The analogy this fantastic tale provides for the One Ring's history suggests the *unnatural* character of a wish; invisibility is a perversion of the natural state of things, and is associated with evil and disorder. In another way, we can say that power destroys or brutalizes its possessor, for the magic ring apparently cannot be used for good; it is a force beyond man which he can only mishandle. But the special power of the One Ring—to give invisibility—is developed by Tolkien from the simple experience of Bilbo in *The Hobbit* into the death-dealing fatality of *The Lord of the Rings* in part to remind us of its mythic precedents and dangers.

The One Ring, then, symbolizes earthly wealth and power. It symbolizes the dangerous ambiguity of power, and the long history of man's attempts to control it—and himself. It represents his wish for goods, ends, not fitting to his nature and the world of which he is a part. The Ring is also a force in itself, falling from Isildur's finger, turning of its own will when Frodo begins his mission.

A "thing" with a will of its own, the Ring can stand for man's loss of his own power of choice to the forces of evil that seek to turn him into a slave, a will-less machine which functions by the command of external orders. For created beings in Tolkien's world have feelings, desires, a sense of the past, take pleasure in smoking tobacco (at least, hobbits do), will risk their lives for a great cause. They are more complex, more difficult, more willful than those who seek power over them wish. The Dark Lord would like to turn such beings into things, and Tolkien suggests the potential for such a reduction of the spirit in the struggle of that piece of gold, the One Ring, to assume the volitional power of a created being. Indeed, the trees that speak and walk, the faces glimmering under the swamp waters of the Dead Marshes, the mountain that tries to destroy the Company of the Ring with its blizzards—these are all instances of "things" coming to unnatural life as evil gains power over the world.

For the Ring is also Fate, the seemingly inevitable force of life itself driving the world toward chaos. History is in one sense the record of man's accomplishments, a sometimes haphazard and sometimes closely ordered collection of memories and books which may be searched for its secrets. History can come to man's aid in the present. But it can also become a power for destruction of the imaginative life; "the Shadow of the Past" lies heavily over Middle-earth in *The Lord of the Rings*, and even in *The Hobbit*. In the former, it is the recurrence of evil from age to age: the Witch-King of an earlier period becomes Sauron, the Dark Lord who threatens the end of Gondor and the Shire. In the latter, the Dwarves' treasure has attracted a dragon, Smaug, who drives them from their kingdom and upon whom they must be revenged. The past never dies; it keeps coming forward into the present, and demanding response, decision, courage, perhaps death. Thus the Ring symbolizes the cyclic nature of the Quest, as hobbits and men set out to deal with this Shadow, and return.

Tolkien has been careful to set the circular pattern of history in an even larger context: that of the *downward* movement of time toward a final catastrophe. The world is running down: greater beings than now live in Middle-earth ruled in the past; the elves are in the process of passing away into mere memory; the men of Gondor were spiritual giants who built the great cities of Westernesse that stand in ruins about the forest; all agree their blood is faded and thin in their descendants. Everywhere in their travels, the Fellows of the Ring come upon re-minders of the great deeds and beings of the past when the world was closer to its beginning and therefore closer to its source in the beauty and truth of its Maker. Its decline is inevitable, as age follows age. Its end may be happy, an apocalypse and a renewal, rather than dismal—the kind of renewal achieved at the end of *The Lord of the Rings* when Sauron and his works are destroyed. But Tolkien makes us feel the press of time upon the questors who from day to painful day move closer to Mordor; or who arrive in the very last moment to raise the seige of Minas Tirith. At that moment in *The Return of the King*, the dawn breaks and a rooster somewhere in the shadows of Time crows, defining the inevitable progression of the hours. Fate is the shape the world of the hours takes and which the One Ring also symbolizes in its own history.

The Ring gives its possessors power according to their "stature," and if they are very weak, it controls them. The Gollum is destroyed by his desire for it, and even mortal men are not strong enough, and in seeking power they must inevitably be destroyed by it. Even those with some kind of supernatural virtue are afraid of it. But in con-nection with this moral and spiritual problem, Tolkien has provided a structural place for the Ring in his trilogy in a very interesting way. The Ring can be seen as whatever one wishes it to be; it is a metaphor, an image, in which we read ourselves. Hence its power over its owners according to their strength and weakness. And Tolkien tells us this is true of its maker, the Dark Lord, as well. Sauron "let a great part of his own former power pass into it, so that he could rule all the others. If he recovers it, then he will command them all again, wher-ever they be. . . ." Frodo's task is to save the One Ring from returning to its maker, and to destroy it in the elemental fires from which it was made in the Cracks of

Doom. After many trials Frodo succeeds, not entirely through his own volition, and when the One Ring vanishes with the Gollum into the flames, Sauron's kingdom and all his efforts to conquer Middle-earth are overthrown. The army of the Allies can only stand in helpless wonder as the Dark Lord's castles fall, the barriers of Mordor are overturned, Mt. Doom erupts in destruction, and the Dark Lord and his creatures vanish into the sky. This apocalyptic experience, the product of imaginative vision, finally, takes place exactly because power is rejected as an end in itself by the forces of good, and this affirmation of goodness and civilization is coupled with Sauron's mistake in giving his power to the Ring. He staked all his power upon a thing, an object, and while its recovery would have completed the circuit so that all energy would flow through his control, the loss of the Ring, its annihilation as a created work of art in the fires of chaos, destroys this last bit of the puzzle, and all crumbles of its own weight. It is typical of evil that it is not imaginative, not flexible, but rigid, narrow, simplistic in its vision of life and of itself.

The narrow circle of the Ring typifies in its form the solipsistic vision of evil beings. But Tolkien has also approached the concept behind the One Ring in an interesting way for an historian of words. The One Ring is "magical" in that it represents its maker's power; in rhetorical terms it is a "synechdoche," that is, a part of a thing which stands for the whole. When we say, "Count noses," we mean to count all the people with noses who are present. And so with the Ring, which, quite literally, "stands for" Sauron's total power. This use of synechdoche appears frequently in magic: toenail parings or the blood from a vein will give the witch power over their original owner. This use of synechdoche in a literal or magical way appears not only in magical "things"; it is the connection between magic spells, secret names, words of power, and their owners. Often, men or animals have secret names given them by spirits, and to know this secret name is to gain power over a man, for his own power or "virtue" is incorporated in it. The High Priest of the Israelites wears the secret name of God, which must never be known or spoken, "hidden" in the design of his ceremonial breast-plate. Disguise and mystery are essential to the religious experience. But, more importantly, to know the name of the Living God is to seek to rival his power. And so with names in fairy-stories. When the peasant's daughter learns the name of the gnome that plagues her, she calls him "Rumpelstiltskin" and he vanishes. Conversely, by giving names to the animals as they passed before him in the Garden of Eden, Adam identified their natures or powers, and so asserted his dominance over them. And perhaps the most famous assertion of the connection between a "thing" and its name or spiritual nature occurs at the start of the Gospel of St. John, where the writer announces that "In the beginning was the Word, and the Word was with God, and the Word was God." Behind the identification of the thing and the Word lies the concept of man's ability to evoke the essential meaning of existence by naming it. In the first chapter of this Gospel, we are told that John the Evangelist, who came before Christ to announce his coming, spoke of the Word giving power in this world:

But as many as received him, to them gave he power to become the sons of God, even to them that believe on his name: . . .
And the Word was made flesh, and dwelt among us . . . full of grace and truth.

These references suggest the long tradition of words *containing* as well as merely representing the objects which they identify. Indeed, one could argue that religion is based upon just such an identification between the observed works of God and the God who made them, and so with the names or words that describe Him and His creation. And, obscure as it may seem, this deeply religious sense of the Word and its power appears in magic and in fairy-stories when hidden truth must be revealed. Then, with a word, illusion is exposed and shattered: Ali Baba opens the cave of the Forty Thieves; Gandalf, the closed doors into the Mines of Moria by speaking the "right word," for the doors are "governed by words."

55

Words and Rings share, then, in the same power: the identification of essence or truth which until revealed, lies hidden in the twists and turns of the seemingly firm world seen with our eyes and touched with our hands, the bird that is really an angel.

It is the principle behind this identification which Tolkien employs to such good effect when, with the destruction of the One Ring, Sauron's world is destroyed. By extension, the Ring *is* the Dark Lord's power, even though, in another way, it is only the *symbol* of his power. In creative fantasy, the symbol and the "thing" are identified; the part of a thing stands for the whole. And so, just as Sauron attempted to reduce life to the simplistic level of his own being, the destruction of the Ring of Power reduces his empire to a voice wailing away on the wind. The simplicity of Tolkien's device is like the conclusion of fairy-stories. Tolkien is relying, as does the teller of fairy-stories, upon our faith, our "Secondary Belief," in this instant transformation of the world. And our faith is supported by the complex nature of the Quest seeking this end; by our faith in the characters who make this journey; by our confidence in the values of an imagined world beyond this real one. The Ring, paradoxically, is its own destruction, and that this is so is expressive of an ultimately *religious* vision of reality which has its source, finally, in Tolkien's confidence in words and their power. For, structurally, the Ring is also a "word," an image, a metaphor for its evil maker, and the creator of a successful Secondary World. The concept behind this use of a single object to destroy evil, its own parent and source, is that behind all magic and religion, one might say: life is single and purposeful, and so its various parts are not only interrelated and carefully ordered toward some end, but they also can stand for each other as in an analogy one thing can stand for another. A Word, like the One Ring, can both "stand for" something else, and possess the power of all things in itself. And so with a myth like *The Lord of the Rings*, a "fantasy" which operates in the same way: at its conclusion we have a glimpse of that "Joy" Tolkien finds revealed at the end of all fairy-stories, all successful journeys, all books. Through analogy, the devices of rhetoric, of storytelling, *The Lord of the Rings* becomes an account of our own lives in the Primary World and their end in Joy. Ultimately, what Tolkien is about is the depiction of the perfectability of Man, and in our imaginative involvement in this fantasy, we move further toward perfection.

But it must be emphasized that our response to *The Hobbit* or the Trilogy is not to words for themselves. We respond to the felt presence of the Secondary World they create. Our search for "moral and emotional Truth" is immediate; in Tolkien's writing we believe in the world he makes because he offers us an "escape" (in his sense) into imagination by making us "feel" the details of that world and know the characters and the landscape intimately. If we were set down by a broad, rather slowly moving, grey-green river flowing south toward a distant range of mountains, we would know without being told by any of the strange inhabitants along its banks that it was the Entwash, so successfully has Tolkien sketched in its nature and location with a few brief words. And behind those words, or images of the Entwash, lies the myth which gives them purpose in *The Lord of the Rings* and which they support and advertise, in turn. It is to the nature of this myth and the traditional literary antecedents for Tolkien's version of it that we must now turn.

Chapter Two: The Journey to the Interior

Perhaps we can put the fantasy of Tolkien in proper perspective by explaining the basic elements of the myth which he employs and the literary antecedents for his story. As we have said, the basis of *The Hobbit* and *The Lord of the Rings* is the Quest, a heroic journey from the known world into the unknown and return. Here a more specific definition of "myth" is important. A myth is not merely a fiction, a poetic lie. More importantly, it is "a large, controlling image that gives philosophical meaning to the facts of ordinary life; that is, has organizing value for experience." [8] For ideas to be useful to us, they must appear not as abstractions but as "pictures," images, to which we attach our feelings, our will to believe, our "primal desires," as well as our thoughts. We wish to believe in ultimate values, Truth and Perfectability, for instance, but these terms mean nothing unless we can know them "in action," as images with which we can live in our own personal worlds. Ideas must appear in forms of some kind. A "large, controlling image," for example, would be that of Christ upon the cross; basic to the Christian religious commitment, such an image "gives meaning" to a Christian's life, organizes experience for him. The crucifixion is a metaphor for the spirit given bodily form, and so speaks to the Christian believer of the transcendental nature of the Primary World. This image is not only an analogy for the Christian life; it is also moral in its statement about standards of conduct, the purposes of God. Thus, we can say that this metaphor makes life meaningful to those who believe in it.

Myth, thought of in this way, provides us with statements about Truth which are emotional and imaginative, rather than rational. Belief is not to be analyzed by the mind, but felt by the heart. And behind this concept lies the nature of man himself, a being who wishes to believe in life and who has sought commitment through the creation of myths throughout his civilized life. The great myths have to be associated, in turn, with religious conviction; they are usually about the most basic, eternal human experiences, and as the story of Christ suggests, they illustrate the activity of the Divine in this world. "The very essence of myth," it has been said, is "that haunting awareness of transcendental forces peering through the cracks of the visible universe." [9] A myth can be a representation of divine power at work in the world; or it can be a way of invoking that power by representing it in action, as magic functions by analogy to "realize imagined wonder." And so with words, which take their meaning from the hidden life they indicate by describing or naming. Like the myths they describe, words are the statement of man's basic nature and his primary relationship to the universe whose meaning he seeks with their aid. And we can say, too, that myth can take the place of religion in that it creates belief in the world's ultimate

59

value. It may be for this reason that Tolkien's *Lord of the Rings* is read so widely today: the Secondary Belief which his creative ability inspires shares the organizational power of religious faith. And finally we must add that the great myths are communal in their meaning, believed in by a society, a community of like-minded beings who organize their lives around a common image. This aspect of myth must appeal to the members of contemporary society who feel alienated and alone in a culture seemingly without values upon which all its members can agree. And we find this element of myth reflected, in turn, in the myths or fantasies themselves. The "fairy-tale" hero often travels with a band of comrades in search of the Holy Grail or the Golden Bough (although the hero usually ends up a solitary savior), or he returns from a lonely journey to the welcoming arms of his tribe or country.

Hence the task of any good writer of fantasy, Tolkien would say, is to make a myth his readers believe in so fully they can enter the Secondary World there established. It satisfies their primal desires and gives them the necessary sense of "flow" between real and imagined realms. Within the fantasy of *The Lord of the Rings* we can say that the One Ring upon which all depends is a "large, controlling image" not only within the book but within our lives as well, whenever we enter the Secondary World of the hobbits. It has the power of organizing our experience there—and here, in the reader's world. After its discovery by Gandalf, when the fire on Frodo's hearth reveals its hidden nature, the efforts of all those opposing Sauron are aimed at destroying this terrible object before its master can recover it. The commitment of the Fellowship of the Ring to this task is ultimately religious in character, giving its members the courage to carry on their task. In this sense, they believe in the One Ring, but more importantly, in themselves and their ability to withstand Sauron's might, which like the power of good, works upon the mind and spirit. Another myth that might be cited is the history of the men of Westernesse, the mighty predecessors of the men of Gondor who play so large a part in the trilogy. Here the early history of men in Middle-earth is mingled with that of the elves; their deeds now remembered are battles against the early forms of Sauron; or romantic legends about the love of Beren son of Baranhir and Luthien Tinuviel daughter of an elvish king "who cast down even the great enemy from his throne, and took from his iron crown one of the three Silmarils, brightest of all jewels. . ."; or the translation of a hero like Earendil to the heavens as a constellation of stars. The history of the men of Westernesse has been forgotten save as it was recast as legend or myth; their kingdom on earth has shrunken to a few cities on the southern coast; the once great capital of Arnor now lies beneath a grassy mound in the far north. But the courage and the beauty of these early civilizers remain behind in stories providing inspiration for their embattled descendents.

Again, these legends from the heroic past lead to prophetic fulfillment in the present. Aragorn is the heir to the men of Numenor or Westernesse, and he has wandered the hills as a Ranger guarding the frontiers of civilization until the time comes for him to claim the throne of his fathers. Legend has promised that the kings will return to Gondor, and Aragorn carries with him the Sword that was Broken, the sword which failed in an early battle with evil and which has been preserved by the heirs of a legendary hero until the time comes to mend it and carry it into battle again. Even the One Ring is connected with the recovery of the kingdom: it had belonged for a time to Isildur, who cut it from the Dark Lord's finger in battle. Called "Isildur's Bane" (the "cause" of Isildur's destruction), the Ring is found again as prophesied, and when it reappears the Sword that was Broken again appears among men. Aragorn has lived on the promises of time, and now steps forward to fulfill these promises. For the destruction of Sauron is complemented by the Return of the King, and Aragorn, purged through trial and battle, becomes King Elessar: "Tall as the sea-kings of old, he stood above all that was near; ancient of days he seemed and yet in the flower of manhood; and wisdom sat upon his brow, and strength and healing were in his hands, and a light was about him" (III, 304).

Here Tolkien's reliance upon the kind of antique phrase-ology we associate with Biblical or fairy-story kings suggests the new king's power and its source: the lineage of his ancestors whose promise from the past is fulfilled in their descendant. He is a mythic king: all worthy kings in fantasy are taller (or seem to be taller) than others; all seem to embody wisdom; they possess the power to heal by laying their hands on the sick; they often glow with an inner light. The discovery of the True King, the Lost Prince, the Sleeping Princess, is a basic theme in fairy-stories, a myth that argues for truth being at last found out, and right reasserting its dominion—in the form of "a large, controlling image." And we should notice that in the descriptions of the King Elessar Tolkien has borrowed from the conventions of heroic description traditional in our culture. As with the image of the One Ring, the recognition and crowning of the True King is an organizing element in the imagination of the community, and the appearance of this image in the Secondary World of *The Lord of the Rings* corresponds to our own interest in such myths in the Primary World.

The Return of the True King is one of the central myths of the Trilogy. We believe in it because it evokes, in Tolkien's skilled hands, our own faith in the recovery of Truth and the revelation of meaning in experience. Other myths occur in these fantasies; the mythic is essential to Tolkien's creative work. In *The Hobbit*, the dwarves, mythy characters themselves, live on the strength of their own history; the existence of ancestral treasure guarded by a dragon animates their desire for vengeance and carries Thorin Oakenshield's band forward to recover their ancestral country. Again, in *The Lord of the Rings*, the ents —those wonderful walking, talking trees, themselves fantastic—preserve their own myth in the hoped-for rediscovery of the ent-wives, who went out of the forest to plant crops in the land to the east of Anduin and never returned. A minute parable of the division between peoples who gather food from the wild and those who cultivated it, the ents' loss of their wives gives them a myth to dream upon. But the "large, controlling image" for the ents is the life in the trees they care for, shepherds of the forest who remember the days when there were *real* forests

62

stretching over Middle-earth, not the few fragments like Fangorn and Mirkwood left behind.

But the principle mythic element to which all the others are related is the Heroic Journey or Quest. This central image in *The Hobbit* and *The Lord of the Rings* provides the moral and structural framework for both fantasies. More fully and complexly developed in the latter work, the Quest is a journey to the "center of life," to the interior of the world where the ultimate meaning of existence lies hidden from mortal men. In this sense, the journey the hero of a quest makes is from ignorance to understanding, or from imperfection to perfection, or from innocence to experience (or even from experience to innocence). It can be seen as a search, perhaps for an object precious to the society from which the searcher comes. Perhaps for the chance to destroy an evil enemy. Perhaps for enlightenment, that "regaining of a clear view," of which Tolkien speaks. But in any mythic Quest, the adventures the hero experiences quickly take on moral and spiritual significance: the Journey becomes a metaphor for man's inner life.

Usually, the Hero of the Quest, who represents his community, must leave his family and friends, and set off into an unknown, alien country. There, after adventures that are actually trials or tests of his physical or spiritual qualities (or both), the Hero obtains the Object of the Quest, and then returns to his own country, either with the prize or with the history of its destruction. An example from Greek mythology is Jason, who, in command of the Argonauts, sails to the far country of Colchis to secure the Golden Fleece, and there kills the dragon guarding this treasure before returning with it to his homeland. Another quest-hero is Orpheus, the singer-poet, who descends into the Underworld after his dead wife, Euridice. There, after playing for the king and queen of the dead, he secures Euridice's return to the upper world. Both myths, however, illustrate the ambiguous nature of such journeys; they can result in unexpected consequences: Jason must bring back with him the king's daughter, Medea, an unfortunate bargain, as it turns out, for in her jealousy she kills their children. Orpheus cannot resist looking back at Euridice as she follows behind him on the path out of Hell, and according to the bargain struck, she must return permanently to the Underworld. Man is not always master of the elemental forces he seeks to possess.

On the whole we can say these things about the Hero: He usually represents the virtues and weaknesses of his society, and they are tested in his person during the Quest. Sir Gawain in the medieval poem *Sir Gawain and the Green Knight*, takes with him on his journey the knightly virtues of King Arthur's court: courage, honor, chastity, and the rest. Their failure to support him in his final test is a sign of his humanity and their necessity. Further, the Hero is usually more than human: he may possess superhuman strength like Beowulf, who kills sea monsters with his bare hands; or he may gain supernatural aid, like Perseus, who kills the gorgon, Medusa, and with her head, the sight of which turns viewers to stone, saves Andromeda from a sea-serpent. Actually, Perseus was the son of Zeus and Danae, and so half-divine in his birth. It is customary for heroes to be greater than human, though not always the children of the gods. Nevertheless, in the precedents for Tolkien's fantasies we are looking at, a little supernatural aid is not unwelcome.

But sometimes this aid comes unexpectedly, along with the divine command to undertake the Quest. For often, the Hero is a younger son of the king, rather than the eldest and most obvious choice, and the Quest is not sought but given to him, that divine purposes may be fulfilled. David is anointed as God's chosen king of the Israelites, over his elder brothers, and without seeking the appointment. In fairy-stories it is often the youngest son who wins the princess, a success story illustrating not only the triumph of innocence and essential purity over maturity and experience, but also the power of God or the elemental directors of life to choose whom they wish to perfect their work. For the initiation of the Quest lies in disruption of the Primary World, the habitual patterns of action men are accustomed to, and the beginning of a new pattern in the community. Hence it should be the second son, not the heir to the established throne, who opens up this new world. Finally, the Hero rarely chooses to undertake the Quest himself; rather, he is chosen, like Jonah who did not wish to go to the wicked city of Nineveh at all. The Hero is the only one who can carry out God's commands, or make his way through the briars to the side of Sleeping Beauty. In this sense the Quest must often be undertaken by someone whose unwillingness is a clue to his election: God or Fate or the supreme power whose purposes are served manifests power through a selected instrument. But the determinism is played down in fantasy with a Christian background because of the traditional Christian emphasis upon the choices for God or the Devil along the Road of Life, choices the responsible soul must make for himself.

If we are to recognize the Quest as a moral journey, we must have moral decisions, which are ruled out if a supreme being makes the decisions for the Hero. Often, the Hero may receive divine aid, but he is usually a human being whose human frailty is all too evident when he stands, alone, uncertain before the two forks of a road— one broad and well-worn and leading over a pleasant countryside to what seems a pleasant palace gleaming attractively in the distance; the other, narrow, overgrown, soon lost among the dark trees of a mysterious forest. Either as Christians or as experienced readers of fantasy, we should expect that fair appearance will disguise the reality of the damned: the broad leads to Hell, and the narrow path to that "strait" gate through which only a few pass to Heaven. But the Hero does not know as he stands making his choice, nor can we always distinguish the two ways: he provides an analogy for all of us throughout life. Thus the Quest is a satisfying theme for fantasy because it provides a formal structure which invites moral interpretation: the Hero "perfects" himself— increasing in physical strength, gaining faith after despair, proving his worthiness to rule the kingdom—through his encounters with strange characters and amazing adventures. These encounters challenge him to be more than he had thought lay in his power; and just as his nature is stretched and perfected, so our imaginations must reach out to accommodate giants and dragons, lovers and angels, encountered along the way.

The adventures, then, must necessarily be painful, frightening, often defeats, for the Hero seeks knowledge or truth, and this end can be arrived at only with trial in the Primary World: Suffering, says William Wordsworth, "shares the nature of infinity." In fantasy, suffering enlightens and expands because fantasy reveals the dual nature of the world; the Hero moves painfully through the landscape of appearance into that of reality. In fact, the Hero must sometimes "die" to the real world in order to know the other, or to show it to us. We find this in myths based upon the cycle of the seasons when the "birth" of Summer is preceded by the "death" of Winter. Or in myths based on the growth and decay of vegetation and the crops necessary for life in agrarian societies. Seeds buried in the earth must "die" to produce the new life of the seedling; or lie dormant under the snow waiting for the spring. The classic example of this pattern, of course, is the death and resurrection of Christ, whose crucifixion provides an analogy for all the paradoxes of life rising out of death in the Primary World. Our participation as readers in this journey lies in the development of our imaginations, and the experience of Joy at such recovery.

For in the end, the Hero usually returns to us, to his people, having risen from the dead, and bringing with him the promise of recovery, of spiritual health, for us all. It is this recovery which Tolkien describes in "On Fairy-stories" when the lost prince is found, when the wicked stepmother is thwarted, when the beautiful can marry each other, when the ugly are banished. When, in other words, the Hero returns with the golden apples, the magic ring, or the secret name, and everything in life can again bloom, come out of hiding, unite, reproduce. The mythic scene should end in fertility and affirmation, in Joy, for the triumph of the soul over evil always finds its reflection in the external world. The recovery of health, then, of which Tolkien writes, is the realization of the perfected self, a metamorphosis in which the change to perfection is not alteration but development, completion, of what was already there: the True Prince is not created anew, but revealed.

Myths, in this way, capture our power to believe in

an ordered, purposive universe through the images in which their story is told. In the form of the Quest, a myth confirms our faith in ultimate realities while testing that faith through the trials of the hero's journey. Finally, myth as written or told by a sub-creator, must convince us of the hero's power to do something for himself, to make responsible decisions. But we must also feel that larger powers are at work behind the scenes, testing and guiding, and the end of the journey must touch us with awe at the sense of some larger plan in the universe, as well as with Joy at the traveler's safe return. It is in part for this reason that most myths or fairy-stories do not spend much time developing the character of the hero: the analysis of his character which we have come to expect from the novel as it has grown up through the past two hundred and fifty years is not important to a mythic vision where the Quest itself is the major theme. The traditional stages on the journey; the hero's struggle with enemies encountered along the way; the sense of his people waiting for his return; the glimpses of divine purpose behind events—these are emphasized. It is a plan for the world which issues in action that makes myths valuable to us, rather than the internal problems of a particular individual.

Tolkien relies on this pattern of myth in telling his story, but he modifies the conventions of the form for his own purposes. Thus he chooses for his heroes unexpected figures, as tradition requires, in this case, hobbits, who do not even figure in the lineage of the people of Middle-earth as recited by the great memory-bank, Treebeard. Frodo and Bilbo are the "second sons" who are overlooked by the powerful until suddenly they are chosen, against their wills, to go on their respective Quests. Neither are warriors or the descendants of kings; but they learn to fight with swords, to struggle in the dark against physically stronger enemies, and to make decisions which reflect moral truths. But we do not feel that the hobbits are simply puppets acting out the purposes of fate or the gods. Tolkien gives us in the character of Frodo, certainly, the picture of a hobbit making decisions about what he can do and cannot do which lead to development in his nature: Frodo is a different individual at the conclusion of *The Lord of the Rings* than when we first meet him living quietly in the secluded life of the Shire. One important element in the Trilogy, in fact, is Tolkien's adoption of an interest in character development exemplified in traditional novels. We can see this particularly in comparing the figure of Frodo with his uncle, Bilbo, in the earlier and simpler book, *The Hobbit*, where the Quest demands certain moral decisions by the older hobbit—how to use the Arkenstone, for instance, to betray Thorin and distribute the dwarves' treasure among all who deserve a part—but Tolkien does not give a close examination of Bilbo's motives and his decisions, as he does in presenting the inner life of the Hero, Frodo. Another important modification of the usual form of the myth lies in the necessity of destroying the desired treasure, the One Ring, rather than obtaining it. But otherwise, we have a fairly traditional mythic cycle operating in Tolkien's fantasy: the journey of the hero into unknown country and his return, a journey or quest which turns a narrative of adventures into a ritual Adventure.

A myth, then, is a story of how man makes wonder manifest in this world, and in describing how man's power operates to accomplish this, the myth becomes an instrument of power itself. In the myth man triumphs over the natural world, defying the laws of time, of space, in his revelation of symbolic meaning in trees and birds, in the passage of the seasons, in his descent into the underworld, contrary to all natural law, and his return from the dead. In a myth the imagination reorders Nature, and makes it produce hidden, spiritual meaning. It is important to point all this out because Tolkien has relied in part on past versions of the basic archetypal myth of the Quest, and in part on his own variations. We have, for instance, a typical hero in the person of Aragorn, the disguised king who, after trial in the wastes and woodlands of Middle-earth, returns to lead his people to victory over the Enemy. But the hobbits have no precedents in ancient lore, save as one or another characteristic is borrowed from fairy-stories about "little people" or the Tale of Peter Rabbit. Tolkien's imaginative synthesis makes them unique.

The fictional world of the hobbits is that of the romance, a term applied to adventure stories or fairy tales of which the Quest is the organizational principle. The term "romance" should immediately suggest that element of "wishful thinking" which Tolkien describes as "primal desire"; it is in romances that we meet the dragons and heroes of our dreams. Hence the romance setting is usually in a distant country where we can believe fantastic things happen, in Beyond the Sea or Never-Never Land, some place strange to the tale's audience and so demanding that the imagination stretch to comprehend this new vision. Furthermore, the setting may be dreamlike, and the causality, the "why" things happen, non-realistic in relation to the Primary World. This is the storyteller's device to make us read events for their imaginative or symbolic implications: they take place in the mind or in the soul. Thus in Spenser's *Fairy Queen*, the Hero, The Red-Cross Knight, encounters strange, perverse figures or personifications representing such obstructions on the Christian path as Error (a ghastly half-woman, half-serpent) and Lucifera, Queen in the House of Pride, and the giant, Orgoglio, who is Pride himself. But the order of his encounters is moral and theological, and he passes through an adventure with Despair before coming to the House of Holiness where he sees the city of God, the heavenly Jerusalem. Among other strange phenomena, "natural" only within the setting of the romance, he finds speaking trees in which souls have been shut up; and he fortuitously falls into the Well of Life during his battle with the Dragon of all dragons (Satan). In a romance or fairy-story, the spiritual or imaginative meaning of a tree or a city or a well shines through the forms of the Primary World; and the successful sub-creator makes this dream landscape visible to the imaginative eye. And the order in which giants and dragons is encountered is determined by the inner logic of the mind or soul.

The heroic geography through which the hero journeys is always lovingly described by writers who, like Tolkien, find the Primary World beautiful, and available for imaginative ordering. Usually the essential scene is pastoral or of the wildwood, where men are not confined to city streets but wander from one country to another: the people farm in one, and hunt in another, both depending upon the ordering of nature for a living, but the total picture ends up varied, a symbolic patchwork of field and forest, castle and farm. Typical is the countryside of *Sir Gawain and the Green Knight*, wherein Sir Gawain travels from the court of King Arthur into the forest in search of the Green Knight. The life at Arthur's court is one elaborate ritual, elegant and artificial. The forest is wild, disordered, untamed by man, filled with monsters, savage giants, wildmen who attack Sir Gawain. But at last he comes to another castle in this alien wood where the court carries on the same traditions as in King Arthur's. And each day Sir Gawain stays in this castle (which turns out to be that of the Green Knight) the lord is out hunting—first the deer, then the boar, and finally the fox. The hunts of each day are described at length; they symbolize man's ordering of life in the wildwood: the deer, for instance, must be hunted for food, but man's conservation of the available supply also suggests his sense of responsibility for the life about him. More importantly, this is the civilized imagination at work. And the author's love of the natural world appears in the care with which he describes the hunt, the pursuit of the deer or fox, the treatment of the prey.

Tolkien, too, pays close attention to the detailed geography of Middle-earth, and to the way trees grow or seem to walk and speak. This love for the Primary World is shared by elves and hobbits and ents in the Secondary World; they not only admire their respective natural homes, they guard them. Indeed, the ents are "Shepherds of the Trees," tending their charges in the depths of Fangorn Forest like sheep. Tolkien, like a good Secondary Creator, can make the landscape do whatever he wants, so far as its contribution to the meaning of the Quest is concerned. The Shire, in which the Quest begins in both *The Hobbit* and *The Lord of the Rings*, is plain English countryside, a gentle pastoral of farms and hedgerows, gardens and hobbit-holes, hilly here and marshy there; in short, a gentle, unassuming country in the backwater of history where the hobbits "plied their well-ordered business of living," heeding "less and less the world outside where dark things moved, until they came to think that peace and plenty were the rule in Middle-earth and the right of all sensible folk. . . . They were, in fact, sheltered, but they had ceased to remember it" (I, 24–5).

The Shire is "civilized" country, the familiar landscape of childhood where we lived protected from the outside world about which we knew and cared very little. But when the hobbits begin their journey to the east with the One Ring, Tolkien moves them through a landscape that begins to take on the symbolic undertones of birth and the consequent discovery of other worlds. Thus, Frodo looks back at his homeland:

> . . . they looked back and saw the lamps in Hobbiton far off twinkling in the gentle valley of the Water. Soon it disappeared in the folds of the darkened land, and was followed by Bywater beside its grey pool. When the light of the last farm was far behind, peeping among the trees, Frodo turned and waved a hand in farewell.
> "I wonder if I shall ever look down into that valley again," he said quietly (I,107).

This is conventionally sentimental, a picture familiar to all of us who have ever left homes which, in a sense, we will never see again, our journeys will have changed our perceptions so. And Tolkien follows this description later with a landscape symbolic of the "birth" of the hobbits into new life and of the dangers of the adventures ahead. Frodo and his friends must pass through the Old Forest on their way to the house of Elrond in Rivendell. The trees in this ominous wood are carefully but generally described, and at the same time, given certain meaningful possibilities:

> Looking back they could see the dark line of the Hedge through the stems of trees that

71

> were already thick about them. Looking ahead
> they could see only tree-trunks of innumerable
> sizes and shapes: straight or bent, twisted, lean-
> ing, squat or slender, smooth or gnarled and
> branched; and all the stems were green or grey
> with moss and slimy, shaggy growths (I, 157).

Here Tolkien does not wish to single out any particular
tree, but to suggest the ominous nature of the forest and
the journey the hobbits must make through it. Obviously
something terrible will happen in this place where the
hobbits must leave the comforting familiarity of the Shire
for the first time. Tolkien prepares for this interpretation
by Merry's description of the Old Forest as a "haunted"
place where the "trees do not like strangers. They watch
you." Here the legendary past begins to touch the travelers, as it comes alive in the twisted vegetation of reality.
Tolkien increases our apprehension by reminding us of
literary or mythic precedents for the Old Forest's existence
in the trilogy. The theme is introduced of the return to
some distant country known, as it were, before birth.
The entrance to the forest is described as a "tunnel"
which "went sloping gently down into the ground. It had
walls of brick at the sides, which rose steadily, until
suddenly they arched over and formed a tunnel that dived
under the Hedge and came out in the hollow on the
other side."

The journey is to be a "birth" into another world,
perhaps into the fantasy world of the unconscious, the
"Wonderland" Alice finds when she falls down a rabbit-
hole and is lost among the mysterious tunnels and
chambers of Lewis Carroll's dream-country. But this
is also the traditional forest in which the self seeks its
identity; Sir Gawain's journey through the monster-filled
forest of "North Wales" takes him to the Green Knight's
beautiful castle in which his knightly virtues will be tested
by the seductive wife of the enchanter. This is also the
"selva oscura," the "dark forest" in which Dante loses
his way at the beginning of the *Divine Comedy*, and there
encounters his guide through Hell, Purgatory, and Heaven,
the poet Virgil. The Old Forest seems to be only a col-

lection of trees, but the hobbits feel its watchfulness; the apparently straightforward tracks shift and disappear, or lead in the wrong direction; the trees drop limbs on them, and seem to close in ominously before their steps. Tolkien had used such a forest earlier, in *The Hobbit*, filling it with giant spiders who entangled in their webs the dwarves traveling to the Lonely Mountain. In *The Lord of the Rings* the action is much more subtle, for the threatening old trees represent not an isolated antagonism to the Quest, but are part and parcel of a web of Nature which has been activated throughout Middle-earth by the renewal of Sauron's power.

The hobbits rest at last beneath an immense willow-tree beside the Withywindle, a tree described in some detail to suggest, in the first place, its "naturalness," and yet its potential for more than ordinary vegetable-life.

> Only a gentle noise on the edge of hearing,
> a soft fluttering as of a song half whispered,
> seemed to stir in the boughs above. [Frodo]
> lifted his heavy eyes and saw leaning over him
> a huge willow-tree, old and hoary. Enormous
> it looked, its sprawling branches going up like
> reaching arms with many long-fingered hands,
> its knotted and twisted trunk gaping in wide
> fissures that creaked faintly as the boughs
> moved (I, 164).

The tired hobbits looking up into the tree can "almost hear words, cool words, saying something about water and sleep. They gave themselves up to the spell and fell fast asleep at the foot of the great grey willow" (I, 165). Coupled with their fatigue from the real world, the carefully mysterious "words" the hobbits think they hear suggest the spellbound world they have entered, and gently lead to the unnatural actions of the willow which tries to kill Frodo by knocking him into the water with its root, and Merry and Pippin by shutting them up inside its bark.

The natural world of trees has turned unnatural under the influence of Sauron's growing power, an ugliness inherited from the past of the Old Forest, a potential which all living beings possess. Where nature had been under civilization's control in the quiet Shire, here in the outside world trees take on human characteristics, sing words, try to kill; Tolkien's careful descriptions of this perverted world prepare us for wonders in the context of the everyday. The destructive personality of Old Willow also foreshadows the use of such incidents in the future, for instance in the vision of the faces of dead warriors who long ago fought in the Gladden Fields and now appear under the waters of the Dead Marshes, before the horrified eyes of Frodo and Sam. They see lights floating in the marshes, perhaps marsh gases: "some like dimly shining smoke, some like misty flames flickering slowly above unseen candles; here and there they twisted like ghostly sheets unfurled by hidden hands." Sam falls into the water, and cries out that he sees "dead faces" there. Frodo replies:

> . . . I have seen them too. In the pools when the candles were lit. They lie in all the pools, pale faces, deep deep under the dark water. I saw them: grim faces and evil, and noble faces and sad. Many faces proud and fair, and weeds in their silver hair. But all foul, all rotting, all dead (II, 297).

These are the spirits of the dead who remain in a terrible limbo, a parody of the mythological Elysian Fields where noble spirits go after death. Here the Power of the Past makes itself felt once again in the appearance of the dead and yet not-dead in the desolate wasteland. Tolkien has established a view of nature in which we can believe, because we must also believe in the unnatural. The Dead Marshes are one more stage in the journey to the dead world of Mordor whose desolation of slag-pits and rocks is the landscape of the mind without the transforming power of the Imagination. And it is significant that as they recover from their fright at this sight of the ancient battleground become a graveyard, the hobbits are further terrified by the appearance of a Ringwraith, another of the living dead, a deformed Man:

> They fell forward, grovelling heedlessly on the cold earth. But the shadow of horror wheeled and returned, passing lower now, right above them, sweeping the fen-reek with its ghastly wings. And then it was gone, flying back to Mordor with the speed of the wrath of Sauron; and behind it the wind roared away, leaving the Dead Marshes bare and bleak. The naked waste, as far as the eye could pierce, even to the distant menace of the mountains, was dappled with the fitful moon light (II, 300).

As Frodo and Sam approach the end of the Quest in the wastes of Mordor, the "unnaturalness" of what is left of life increases until finally we meet Shelob the giant spider, and the bloodthirsty orcs who kill even each other. Tolkien gives us descriptions drawn from the landscape of the Primary World that convince us of their "truth," and then adds some fantastic detail to suggest the dream world that lies within it. This is, after all, a journey into the secret, perhaps unconscious, parts of the earth, where Ringwraiths abound. And yet it is also *this* world in which we live, where the "Entwash flows in by many mouths from Fangorn in the west," and the "wind blows from the East there . . . over the Dead Marshes and the Noman-lands. . . ." If we were set down by the bleak hills of the Emyn Muil, which no amount of imaginative power can civilize, we would know exactly where we were, so carefully has Tolkien described the painful journey of Sam and Frodo down their sides, so vividly has he located a map of the place in our heads.

This geography of dream and reality is ultimately moral in its implications, a geography of suffering and trial for the heroic adventurers. It also provides an illustrative analogy for man's conduct in the Primary World: Tolkien's loving descriptions of Middle-earth lead not to the ash-heap of Mordor, but to its renewal as the lands ravished by the raiders of Sauron are returned to their

Garden of Eden condition under the rule of King Elessar. But the deserts of Mordor are the industrial wastes of England and America, natural beauty destroyed by man's thoughtless pollution; the restored Gardens of Ithulien are Nature permitted to be itself again by man's imagination. Tolkien, in other words, uses the country of romance not only to provide a fantastic setting for the Quest; he also provides a parallel with our own time.

It is important to note the similarities and differences in the traditional romance hero and those Tolkien creates. The traditional tale concludes in a goal achieved, a task completed; the hero has won through to the end not only with endurance, but with feats of arms, often pure physical strength, the romance narrative depending less upon psychological development than upon events in the world of action. A good illustration of romance technique that must have influenced Tolkien appears in the late nineteenth-century novels of William Morris. In an industrialized England filling up with slag-heaps and slums, Morris turned back to the medieval setting of *Sir Gawain and the Green Knight* and *The Fairy Queen* for his novels. The world of knights in armor, of famous swords and battles, of castles and church-building, of prayer and allegory—the literary conventions of the medieval world—seems to have an appeal to imaginative writers suffering from any sense of increasing dehumanization in an industrial and commercial society like our own. There are several reasons for this. In the first place, the knight who proves himself on the battlefield with his sword and lance must fight a lonely battle; his strength lies in himself, not in his small place in a massive mechanized army where the complexities of human motives are not relevant. The decisions which such a knightly hero must make about the power he exercises are important. And there are the attractive attributes of such power: the sword with a name like Durendal or Excaliber; the armor of heroes like that of the Red Cross Knight, "oft dinted" from great battles with the forces of evil; the mighty horse of the warrior: all things in personal contact with the hero as the war machines of a later age are not. But the literature of the imagined Age of Knights has also fixed for later sub-creators an image of the knight and his romantic quest as symbols of a meaningful universe. The knight fights for a purpose, a struggle which affirms ultimate meaning in experience. For a writer of the nineteenth century, the Middle Ages must have seemed a period of certainty, when the Church and the State, the Family and Society were welded together in a well-ordered community whose purpose was to serve God. This essentially religious reading of history meant, in turn, that high ideals could be achieved, that battles were worth fighting because ideals did exist to be realized in the Primary World. Literary and artistic tradition had surrounded the brute facts of history with a glamor which they may not have actually possessed, but which was certainly absent from the world of Tolkien and Morris.

Morris' novel, *The Well at the World's End*, can be taken as typical of this vision, and of much that has been said about the nature of the Hero and the Quest. Ralph is the youngest son of the King of Upmeads, a tiny kingdom hidden among the hills. Ralph has no experience in the great world, but he has physical courage and a curious nature, and the desire to prove himself in some worthy task. Although required to stay at home while his brothers seek their fortunes in the outer world, Ralph runs away and ends up on a Quest in search of the Well at the World's End. After many adventures with brigands and lovely women, he does indeed arrive at the Well, drinks of its waters, and returns to scourge his kingdom of evil-doers and reign for many years as The Good King. His journey is not only for himself; his trials of physical and spiritual strength serve the larger purposes of the universe in leaving it a better world for his life there. Ralph's Quest takes on cosmic meaning through Morris' careful alignment of dream and reality, event and symbol.

For instance, logically Ralph should *not* be the son who seeks the Well. But he has been selected by a greater force, by Fate perhaps, for his task; he is given a pair of beads which mark his destiny: "salvation to thee in peril, and good luck to thee in the time of questing," Dame Katherine says upon giving them to him.[10] So Ralph both wills to go upon the Quest and feels himself chosen for it, a combination of choice and fate which must be sustained in successful romance for the reader to believe in the hero and his choices. Ralph takes up the pursuit of the Well because it gives a purpose to this life, and in so doing, he begins the service of his fellow men, who will profit from his experience. The gift of the Well does not come unearned; it must be won after perilous adventures demanding that the hero relinquish his place in the world of power: Ralph travels disguised as an ordinary knight. For Ralph (or Frodo or Aragorn) to turn from humble origins into a great being through magic, say, would subvert the relationship of fantasy with the real world, in which suffering and trial are the basis of experience. The task of the romance writer is to interweave the willed actions of his hero with a suggestion of their fatal or predetermined character; thus Ralph must choose which way to go at a crossroads, but that choice will always be the "right" one in terms of the Quest's larger purposes. And so with the heroes of Tolkien's fantasy, Bilbo and Frodo, who come "by chance" into their historical responsibilities; Bilbo, pursued under the roots of the mountains by the goblins, wakes up in the dark of a tunnel, his head swimming, and "suddenly his hand met what felt like a tiny ring of cold metal lying on the floor . . . It was a turning point in his career, but he did not know it. He put the ring in his pocket almost without thinking." [11] Of course, this is the One Ring which has "accidently" fallen to him, in the way such things happen; as Gandalf explains many years later to Frodo: "Behind that there was something else at work, beyond any design of the Ring-maker. I can put it no plainer than by saying that Bilbo was *meant* to find the Ring. . . ." This potential source of power for the hobbit must be manifest by its new possessor; after smoking a pipe and drawing out his elvish sword, objects suggesting the ordinary and the supernatural elements in Bilbo's life at this moment, he decides to go forward: "Go back?" he thought. "No good at all! Go sideways? Impossible! Go forward? Only thing to do! On we go!" (*Hobbit*, 77). The writer of romance is careful to keep the actions of his creatures in "this world."

And, once again, the heroes of romance need not be very complex figures psychologically or spiritually. In Morris' novel, Ralph must be brave, courteous, reverent —the virtues of the Boy Scout—but most importantly, capable of sustained faith in his task. But Ralph is also innocent in the ways of the world, and so he speaks less with himself and listens more to the characters of knight, hermit or lovely lady whom he meets on his way. Adventures in the beginning of his narrative happen to him; he does not cause them. As he gives himself to the Quest, he becomes more single-minded, less available to the desperate quests of other men who seek their identities in the Primary World. Ralph's kind of innocence, based upon commitment to the Quest, is shown to be a valuable kind of idealism because he can pursue the almost unattainable goal, and still rescue maidens, fight for virtue, reward valor or honesty along his way. The Primary World cannot immediately reward the Hero, and Ralph's simple idealism is in blatant contrast to the greed or lust of others, men typifying the Deadly Sins of medieval theology.

Ralph's Quest takes him through the varied pastoral landscape of the typical romance where towns and castles appear and disappear in traditional fashion. The woodlands are always dark, and bloodthirsty men lurk in the coverts, but they must be entered. The castles may be heavily allegorical; Ralph lives for a time in the House of Abundance whose walls are hung with tapestries depicting the life of the Lady of the Wood Perilous with whom he falls in love. For the traditional figures appear not only in the Hermit and the Knight of the Sun, but also in the two principal women of Ralph's life, the Lady and her rather more human counterpart, Ursula, whom Ralph finally marries after she has accompanied him to the Well at the World's End. Unlike Tolkien, whose Trilogy is virtually sexless, Morris provides moral support for Ralph in his love first for the Lady of the Wood Perilous and then for Ursula. The first is a figure of mystery, of magic; she has already journied to the Well, and returned to rule as a queen and military leader over many lands. High-spirited, beautiful, as we expect from the literary conventions of her kind, she is the supernatural woman-figure for whom men kill each other; her beauty drives them to do evil, and she is herself killed by one of her lovers when she and Ralph have run away into the forest together. The Lady is the more-than-human spirit who guides Ralph's destiny in his passion for her, but who is, in the end, a Belle Dame sans Merci, who lures her lovers into the world of dream, the pursuit of eternal Beauty. Heroes must turn from such pursuit if they are to do good in the ordinary human community. And Ralph falls in love with Ursula, a mere country maid, a symbol of human and familial love set against the passion for supernatural beauty. The connection between the two women in Ralph's life is established in a vision, traditional in medieval romance literature, in which the Lady of the Wood, after her death, speaks to Ralph, telling him that she lives on in her more human successor:

> So it is that I am not dead but alive in the world, though I am far away from this land; and it is good that thou shouldst go seek the Well at the World's End not all alone: and the seeker may find. . . .[12]

And in the vision, the human Ursula appears, saying, "I am a sending of the woman whom thou has loved, and I should not have been here save she had sent me." Ralph awakes in the morning to the life of ordinary men: "and there was stir in the street and the voice of men, and the scent of fresh herbs and worts, and fruits; for it was market-day, and the country folk were early afoot, that they might array their wares timely in the market-place."

The women-figures are contrasting and yet complementary aspects of Ralph's own character: both contribute to the making of his life and to the picture of power which makes *The Well at the World's End* so richly complex a novel. Morris is also emphasizing the love of love, sexuality purified by care for another person; although both the magical Lady of the Wood Perilous and merely human Ursula are necessary to a complete life, the imagination, which can be wild and undisciplined, must come down into the world of reality where the hero exercises his power wisely, as a real human being. And so the Lady becomes the bride and mother, and the Quest which begins in the pursuit of a dream ends in constructive human purposes in the little land of Upmeads to which Ralph and Ursula return. Before they begin the final stage of the journey to the World's End, an ancient Sage (a figure of the Wise Man, like Merlin who advised King Arthur, or Tiresias, counselor of mythological Greek kings, often turning up in fantasy adventures), cautions them that they must make their Quest in the right spirit:

> . . . that if ye love not the earth and the world with all your souls, and will not strive all ye may to be frank and happy therein, your toil and peril aforesaid shall win you no blessing but a curse. Therefore I bid you be no tyrants or builders of cities for merchants and usurers and warriors and thralls . . . But rather I bid you to live in peace and patience without fear or hatred, and to succour the oppressed and love the lovely, and to be the friends of men, so that when ye are dead at last, men may say of you, they brought down Heaven to the Earth for a little while (II, 36).

Tolkien would never express his ideas in quite so conventional a style, but nevertheless Morris' Sage is defining the ethical and social idealism of fantasy reviewed in "On Fairy-Stories." Men are responsible for the Earth; they do not "possess" it, but must respect its beauty and integrity, and that of the living things in it. Power must be exercised in the Earth's defense, to build in the traditional patterns of the ancient community of men. The greater happiness, Ralph explains, is to "hold war aloof and walk in free fields, and see my children growing up about me, and lie at last beside my fathers in the choir of St. Laurence." Love of woman is part of this love of the land, of the vital past, of the family, of life itself, a love symbolized in the romance where Ralph's Quest spreads out over the world in a large, visionary embrace of experience that is imaginative and liberating, though for

Morris it is finally rather middle-class in its conclusions.

And there is the Well itself, the archetypal goal which is less the end than the incentive for Ralph's maturation into the Good King. The Well is said to contain the miraculous properties of saving "from weariness and wounding and sickness; and it winneth love from all and maybe life everlasting" (I, 11). Or, we are also told, the healing waters contain "the Quenching of Sorrow, and Clearing of the Eyes that they may behold." In other words, the Well promises superhuman qualities of the kind defined in Tolkien's term "Recovery": a release from the burden of nature, and from that egotism which presumes knowledge is power to possess other created beings. Later, we learn that long life and renewal or preservation of physical beauty come with drinking the waters. But these more than ordinary results do not make the drinkers into supermen; they remain, as Ralph does, strong and courageous, with more than ordinary human power. The gift of the Well does not come unearned, and Ralph and Ursula's approach to it approximates that of Frodo and Sam to the wastes of Mordor; the deserts at the end of both Quests are symbolic of Nature unkind where Life itself (or the will of Sauron) have laid the earth waste. These deserts are also the barren plains of the heart without love, in which only the spirit of love or the traveler's endurance can sustain him. Ralph and Ursula pass over mountains, fight with a bear, and find in the desert the bodies of others who died seeking the Well. They come upon the Dry Tree with roots in a pool of poisonous water, and here lie more lost pilgrims who were "beguiled" by a vain quest; the pool with its dry tree symbolizes the sterility of those who seek power or wealth or self-aggrandizement at the expense of others. The Well itself lies on the seashore, where man's hand has enclosed a spring with rock, the last earthly place where the imagination of civilized man has made a stay against the oblivion which the surrounding salt ocean promises. In both *The Well at the World's End* and *The Lord of the Rings*, the sea is the place in which individual value and identity will be lost; Tolkien's elves both fear the ocean and are attracted to it, because somewhere on the other side lies the eternal world. But like the orchard or the farm or the church, the carved rocks of the Well are the artful constructions of the imagination which civilizes the desert sands. The waters of the Well are the waters of life which must be used for good, and man must choose to use them so, even after he returns: the words carved on the stone read, in part, "Drink of me, if ye deem that ye be strong enough in desire to bear length of days," the implication being that longer life will continue to be one of work and suffering in the garden of time.

In the end, Morris describes the return of Ralph to his little country as a kind of apocalypse, a renewal of spiritual life like that promised in the Book of Revelation when at the end of time a new heaven and a new earth will appear. This is a vision of perfection, of the best in man and in nature fulfilled. Usually this apocalypse is destructive of the old forms: war, plague, the appearance of an Anti-Christ presage the coming change. And then the metamorphosis into the new form, as our potential for perfection is at last realized. In *The Well at the World's End* the land is cleared of pirates, of evil warriors; the wastes are made to produce food again. The royal family of Upmeads is brought together with the "prodigal Son" Ralph, returning with his knowledge and strength to rule over his own kingdom. The Joy expressed in this cyclic conclusion is expressive of the heavenly Joy Tolkien describes revealed to us, and revealed through the efforts of man. This is the "consolation" of the happy ending, in which Ralph has realized his ideals in the world in which he lives, and his "resurrection" is a denial of "universal final defeat" achieved in his own person.

This reminds us that another element must enter into the calculations of Tolkien's fictional wealth, an element which is contrary to the Christian joy of affirmation identified with the romance. This is the elegaic tone of Tolkien's fantasies, and his emphasis not only upon fulfillment of ideals and achievement of the goal. *The Lord of the Rings* ends with happiness for some, but not for all the principal characters: Frodo, Bilbo, Gandalf and the high rulers of the elves must depart Middle-earth after their Quest is completed and the Age of Men begins. Power must inevitably destroy its possessor, and even though Frodo fights against the One Ring, it wastes him as it did Bilbo, and he cannot stay in the new world ahead. Perhaps more importantly, however, Tolkien suggests the winding-down of the world from age to age, not only in the fatigue of the journeys the Allies must make, but also in the presentation of history as inevitably destructive; the One Ring must be destroyed, but its destruction means the end of the world as hobbits and men, elves and dwarves have known it. The elves must complete their departure from Middle-earth even though Sauron is defeated. And the Men who now rule are lesser men than their ancestors. In the corners of the wilderness lie the bones of lost civilizations, cities buried and forgotten under the grass. The heroes of the past are now but legend, memories for the lore-masters; no man has power to stay the great wave of time. This deep and abiding sense of the coming end of the world lies perhaps even more deeply than Christian joy behind Tolkien's trilogy. He is an author who can make his sense of joy and of fate profitable because they can be played off against each other. Where the romance Quest reveals meaning in the universe, and order which lies behind the experience of the Primary World, another tradition depicts man's struggle to preserve something of civilization for a little while against the dark, perhaps nameless, forces that will triumph over him in the end. This is the tradition of the legendary materials of Northern Europe, the sagas, fairy-stories and elegiac poetry of the period when Norsemen and Saxons were invading the West, bringing with them a poetry which was often a history of their tribal exploits in the dark places of the continent.

In such literature, the sunlit pastures and farmlands, the tapestry-hung castles and open roadways of romance give way to forests inhabited by trolls and monsters, perversions of nature, and to wooden halls that are essentially barracks for warriors whose fires shine for a time against dark enemies before they are extinguished. In this poetry man struggles against monsters, greedy kings, evil counselors, and is doomed to failure at last. In discussing the most famous of all Anglo-Saxon poems, *Beowulf,* Tolkien quotes a line central to its meaning, the theme of fate overwhelming even the strong: "Life is fleeting: everything passes away, light and life together." [13] The emphasis is upon death, upon the brevity of life on earth. The world will not pass into a revelatory apocalypse, but will be destroyed in a reversion to chaos, and neither men nor gods can arrest its descent. There is no Recovery, there is no Joy. In the end there is only man's courage, and his will to struggle against his fate.

Briefly, *Beowulf* divides into two major episodes. The first is the account of the hero himself, stronger physically and spiritually than ordinary men, who comes with a band of loyal warriors to the land of the Danes. He has come to help the Danish king, Hrothgar, destroy a monster, Grendal, which has been ravaging the land, and carrying off Danish warriors from the palace of Herot itself. Beowulf's strength proves equal to the task; after catching Grendal and wrenching off his arm, he pursues him beneath the waters of a pond and destroys the monster and his mother, both hideous descendants of the race of Cain, the first murderer. In the second episode, Beowulf, who has returned to his homeland and finally become its king, is forced in his old age to fight a fire-drake or dragon, very much like the dragon in *The Hobbit.* Although with the help of a companion he successfully kills the dragon, he dies, and is cremated by his tribe in a giant bonfire which signals the end of the world as this warrior people have known it.

There are several points to be made here in relationship to Tolkien's work. In the first place, the hero of *Beowulf* is a warrior who must battle continually with monsters of the land, sea and air, and with men who seek to destroy his people, the Geats. His is a history of violence, in which brute force manifests the will of the gods. And when the gods desert a man, he falls. The long descriptions of Beowulf's battle with Grendal or with the fire-drake suggests an audience which demanded a hero great in arms. In turn, their vision of life was one of conflict between good and evil, man and the devil, a conflict fought in the flesh on a geographically identifiable battlefield. We have met the Good Knight before, in Ralph from Upmeads, and he reappears in medieval trappings—the armored forces of the Allies—in *The Lord of the Rings*. The great battle before the gates of Minas Tirith which turns the tide against the Dark Lord is derived perhaps from the Biblical promise of Armageddon when Christ the Warrior will defeat the armies of Gog and Magog before the Second Coming, but it repeats a traditional vision: evil must be physically resisted, the Devil or Anti-Christ must be slain in the flesh. And so much of the obvious delight Tolkien takes in describing the arming of the warriors of Rohan, of the battles scattered throughout the trilogy, is derived from the literature of a people for whom sword and shield symbolize a way of life. Life is a conflict, and only the strong-armed (and the good swimmer) can pursue Grendal into his pool and there finish him off.

Beowulf is also suitably royal, though again, not a direct descendant of the ruling line. More importantly, he stands by whatever oath he swears, and in the loyalty which he offers the distressed Danish king, or which he commands from his warrior followers, he epitomizes that confidence in himself and his oath which is a faith for the members of a tribe. The group of warriors who pledge themselves to follow him form a family based on strength and fidelity, and so provide a precedent for the Fellowship of the Ring in which the company selected to accompany Frodo south with the One Ring agree to go so far, and Frodo swears to take the Ring to Mordor itself, a promise which keeps him going in desperate moments when he would like to give up. The ethical code of prefeudal loyalty provides the Fellowship with a spiritual and psychological unity, as well. Boromir, the knight from Gondor, breaks his oath when he tries to take the Ring from Frodo and is killed by orcs. The Ring itself is powerful enough to secure the breaking of an oath. But Tolkien is also remembering the history of broken oaths which dot the pages of *Beowulf* and seem endemic in the sagas of the North; loyalty can stand up against the desire for power only in the loyal. The followers of Beowulf who swear to support him also provide Tolkien with the prototype for an essentially masculine world.

Women figure little in the Anglo-Saxon poem, unlike the romance where they seduce and reward, or in Morris' novel, *Journey to the Well at the World's End*. In Tolkien's trilogy, females are few and far between: Lobelia Sackville-Baggins is a comic-strip caricature of greed and narrow-mindedness; Arwen, the daughter of Elrond, is an ephemeral figure from romance who represents the elvish beauty of the past and sews Aragorn a banner for battle in the best romance tradition; Galadriel, the ruler of the elves, possesses power but may not employ it aggressively against Sauron or be destroyed herself. She becomes an inspiration for the Fellowship; her words and the light she gives Frodo help the bearers of the One Ring in dark moments. But she is essentially an inspiring legend, and with the other elves she must pass away across the sea at the end of the Quest. The niece of the king of Rohan, Eowyn, becomes a kind of warrior-maiden, a Brunhilde, who brings down the Black Prince of Sauron's forces in battle, but in the end she renounces her pretensions as a warrior. None of these females plays a large part in the development of the Quest, and we must assume that Tolkien is here referring back to the warrior tradition of northern myth which pitted *men* against evil; it is the man with the sword who must choose to betray his oath or deny his god. Tolkien must have also wished to keep sexuality out of it; Aragorn and Sam marry in the end, and life begins again after the terrible wars, but Frodo and Gandalf and others pass into the west, having sacrificed their personal lives for larger purposes. Beowulf dies alone, save for his faithful follower, Wiglaf, the oaths sworn between men being stronger—and weaker—than sexual bonds.

Finally, the largest contribution to Tolkien's world vision made by these ancient stories is the feeling of doom which pervades them, and the need for men to fight while they can, even though the end is inevitable. Beowulf's "quest" begins with his journey to the Danish court, where he seeks to aid the king. And Beowulf's self-confidence, which he lays on the line like all great warriors, is qualified by the warrior's acceptance of Fate. He tells the Danes:

> "When we crossed the sea, my comrades
> And I, I already knew that all
> My purpose was this: to win the good will
> Of your people or die in battle, pressed
> In Grendel's fierce grip. Let me live in greatness
> And courage, or here in this hall welcome
> My death!" [14]

And this theme of Fate both challenged and accepted is sounded over and over: "Fate will unwind as it must!" (l. 455). The great warrior-hero must not only fight battles with earthly and unearthly beings; he must also accept the warfare of life in which time and fate will finally destroy him. However, he must go on fighting anyway, since in such a world the greatest values are courage, and the will to endure, so long as Fate permits. This courage in the face of imminent death makes the conclusion of Beowulf's journey deeply moving because before the advance of the fire-drake his old body betrays him—but his will to fight is as strong as ever. It is this spirited refusal of Beowulf to give in to evil, his continued assertion of man's power against the dark forces of chaos, that Tolkien has used in his representation of the struggle of the Allies against Sauron. There is always the threat of destructive pride; Beowulf's power can be a threat to the society if he becomes an oath-breaker, or if he actually turns to challenge fate through greed or excessive self-assurance. Man must remember he is but man: ". . . who/In human unwisdom, in the middle of such power,/Remembers that it will all end, and too soon" (ll. 172–4). We see this theme reappear in many places in *The Lord of the Rings*: it is the theme of possessiveness, of thinking we are free of the limits and responsibilities of the world of which our lives are part. [15] This is Saruman, whose pride in his knowledge leads him to side with the Dark Lord. This is Denethor, the Last Steward of Gondor, who thinks with the palentir to compete with the forces of darkness that are already far beyond his control. But for all the dangers of pride, *Beowulf* still says that man must choose: he must not withdraw from battle because his freedom lies in preserving the vision of his freedom.

Evil can come from within, as man's imagination is submerged, imprisoned, in his pride. But it can come from without, unsought, as Frodo finds when the power of the Dark Lord begins to darken Middle-earth, and reach even into the Shire, as Beowulf finds, when a man unknown to him rifles the hoard of the fire-drake, peaceful until then, and sends it out on a rampage which the old warrior must stop. If fire-drakes, or Smaug, did not exist, they would have to be invented. History is not a dead past to be ignored, but reaches into the present, to challenge, to foster, to destroy. The One Ring comes out of the past to Frodo; the treasures buried in the earth in ages long gone by the last man of some forgotten race attract the dragon and bring him, at last, with fire and destruction, into Beowulf's world. Denethor's body is burned on a pyre; a warrior dies in flame. Beowulf's body is burned on the beach, and even as he is consumed and passes into history, he is turned into an "imagined" hero:

> The Geats stayed,
> Moaning their sorrow, lamenting their lord:
> A gnarled old woman, hair wound
> Tight and gray on her head, groaned
> A song of misery, of infinite sadness
> And days of mourning, of fear and sorrow
> To come, slaughter and terror and captivity.
> And Heaven swallowed the billowing
>   smoke (ll.3148–54).

Beowulf becomes the poem *Beowulf*, a record of his own past and of the end of the civilization he defended as best he could, in the future. This brooding sense of impending darkness hangs over Northern myth, and over *The Lord of the Rings*, a vision much more tragic than that suggested by romance literature or by *The Hobbit*. The tragic demands more of man than the romantic because any stay he wins from time, from death, must be fought for, and it is only a "stay," nothing permanent. Even the poems, the myths, the novels that remain as ancient lore will finally vanish, and the imagination can only hope to record such death as it can. This is the legendary death of Arwen Undomiel, King Elessar's queen:

> There at last when the mallorn-leaves were falling, but spring had not yet come, she laid herself to rest upon Cerin Amroth; and there is her green grave, until the world is changed, and all the days of her life are utterly forgotten by men that come after, and elanor and niphredil bloom no more east of the Sea (III, 428).

The flowers beloved by the elves no longer bloom in Middle-earth, and so we know we are in the Age of Men. But Tolkien's sense of history winding down toward an end, even as a new Age takes shape, broadens the scope of *The Lord of the Rings* and makes it into a very different book than *The Hobbit* or other fantasy of its kind.

And it is for this reason that something must be said about the literary history of Tolkien's work because he is writing in a form which uses the historical past for richness and depth in the creation of the Secondary World. He is representing present actions, whether of hobbits or men, which have grown up out of the past, and are continually influenced by it, indeed, often repeat it. And finally, the literary forms Tolkien uses have come from the past of our civilization, for better or worse, and we need to know what he has done with them to create his own Secondary World and make us believe in it. How the imagination has achieved freedom in the past is important to those who wish to find it now. Tolkien is read, in part, because *The Lord of the Rings* argues that freedom can be found, not through rejection of power, but through acceptance of the challenge which it offers to the Primary World.

Chapter Three: The Hobbits in History

The Secondary World of *The Lord of the Rings* is panoramic, many-leveled, and complex in structure; yet all the parts are so carefully related to one another that they describe a grand and simple design. Discussion of precedent myth and fairy-story, even reading *The Hobbit*, does not prepare the reader for the scale of the action and the paradoxical delight in the small things of life, real and imagined, which expand the range of Tolkien's major work and give it power over its readers. The sub-creator, we remember, seeks "the power of making immediately effective by the will the visions of 'fantasy.' " We must see how Tolkien has taken the imagined past described in romance and legend and made it into a new and believable Secondary World—not his "own" exactly, because that would be a possessive and, consequently, destructive act. The visions of fantasy must be given convincing form, and Tolkien, taking the past and turning it in his hands with love and admiration, has made it into a vision of the Primary and the Secondary Worlds and their relationship which is both an illustration of the Enchanter's power and an act of freedom in the Primary World. The fantasist's theme is the moral use of power, and consequently an act of the Imagination describing this power must be moral, as well, since that act, too, is power-filled. Fantasy with its vision of monsters and men, its fabulous adventures, its promise of Joy, helps us escape from possessiveness, by "making something new" and so acknowledging the life in other things: "you will be warned that all you had (or knew) was dangerous and potent, not effectively chained, free and wild; no more yours than they were you" ("On Fairy-Stories," p. 59). Being a man and a subcreator is a difficult task. For man's mind gives him potential power over the living things of the natural world, including his fellow men. He can use his power to free man from the limitations of the body, of society, of the self; from time and death. However, power can also brutalize and destroy him if he misuses it, if he forces other living beings into his particular vision, failing to respect their natural bent and freedom.

Man is constantly in the process of freeing himself from possessiveness. The regaining of "a clear view" of other beings "as things apart from ourselves" is never permanent, never final; exactly as "The Road goes ever on and on" in Bilbo's song, so we can never rest from struggling to secure "a clear view." A halt at some point in the struggle would be impossible, for Tolkien's view of life is one of constant process and perception, and is therefore opposed to the purpose of the One Ring which is to "bind" life, enclose it within its circle forever. Consequently, the record of history, and the basic pattern of fantasy as Tolkien presents it, is a dialectic between the past and the imagination. The past has many weapons. It has time, which is gradually unrolling toward the end of the world and the death of civilization. Time repeats itself over and over so that men become accustomed to its possessive and destructive presence. The past contains acts of dead beings who at some time set in motion events or ideas affecting future generations. The past is not absurd, as the Existentialists maintain, beginning only a moment ago. It lives for all of us in the shapes our civilization takes now; in our ability to think about the present; in the One Ring, for instance, which has found its way down through time because created beings will never stop seeking power. The One Ring "lives" for Bilbo and Frodo to use in the destructive game the past plays.

But the imagination is a weapon too, and if rightly used, can counter and manipulate the past. The love of life which the imagination fosters; the respect for other living things, an imaginative act; the belief in ultimate good and the will to realize it—these are weapons in the inevitable conflict. Perhaps the most important, to return to the activity of the sub-creator, is to make words, a song, a Secondary World giving shape to the Primary World and the events in it, making time into an agent for freedom. In other words, the imagination, which can show us the reality behind appearances, can also take time and the days and events of the past, and counter the threat to our freedom they portend. Gandalf can read the lore of the past and learn from it how to combat Sauron; Frodo can plug away drearily day after day in the long journey to Mt. Doom and so, unexpectedly, thwart the Dark Lord. Samwise can speak elvish words he does not understand, and their power, from far down the centuries, is so great that Shelob retreats, fleeing them and the light of Galadriel, who is far away in Lothlorien. The past lives, and it is the task of the imagination to order it constructively. The imagination, in turn, is positive; it can never be used for destructive (that is, possessive) ends. Those who use their imagination, who live on this earth, are continuously exposed to this dilemma. In a sense the history of man is the history of how he has used his potential for good and evil, and of how past choices have affected the world generation after generation. Man does not escape the demands of the past through fantasy. On the contrary, he chooses (or does not choose) to accept the responsibility of being free which his birth in time imposes on him, and to live or die as freely as he can. It is the congruence of history and imagination that makes *The Lord of the Rings* the effective work it is. Consequently, we shall have to see how Tolkien shapes his Secondary World around these basic elements.

Tolkien uses as his basic structural element the journey or Quest. In *The Lord of the Rings*, the journey is undertaken not by a single hero but by many, representing the living beings of Middle-earth who seek to thwart the power of the One Ring and its maker, Sauron. The various figures who accompany the Ringbearer are all affected by the shape which history has taken at this point; and they respond to the challenge imaginatively, depending on who they are and the history of their race and power. The Quest itself makes two complementary "tracks"; the end of both is freedom. One track is that of Frodo, the Ring-bearer, whose task is to destroy the One Ring, which has come into the history of Middle-earth again. The other track is that of Aragorn, who, with the help of Gandalf, returns as king to the throne of his fathers, and presides over the initiation of the Fourth Age, the Age of Men, in which we live. Structurally, Tolkien represents history moving "down" to the end of one phase, and "up" to the beginning of another. The end of one is required so that the next can begin, and even as Frodo and Sam inch their way alone toward the apocalypse, the vast armies of the Allies against Sauron fight across Gondor to bring the new world into being. This is the dialectic of history, and it means that the Quest has a dual nature, requiring different means for achieving its end: the triumph of life over death, the defeat of the Dark Lord, the return of the King. The dual pattern of the Quest in *The Lord of the Rings* makes that fantasy much more complex than *The Hobbit*, with the single hero, Bilbo, and his journey to the Lonely Mountain. The later work suggests Tolkien's mature ability to see life as more complicated and more tragic than before. Only at the end of the story of Bilbo—when he gives up the Arkenstone and, later, the treasures that fall to his share—do we see Tolkien trying to give significant depth to his portrayal of the hobbit.

Consequently, we must consider the characters who people Tolkien's work before we look at the thematic structure of his great fantasy. An examination of the complexity of the Quest theme in *The Lord of the Rings* shows us that history and the imagination meet there, and their conflict is the basis for everything that happens in this Secondary World. The various races and individuals who appear are defined by their relationship to history and to the power over it which the imagination provides. We must first say something more about what Tolkien means by "history," and note that *The Hobbit* should be included in the discussion since it is part of the "history" of the later work. But, most importantly, we should understand that history is not just the inevitable working out of time in ways beyond man's control. Tolkien shows us in the creation of his characters that our personal decisions make history, too, and that heroism is important. In fact, it is in his definition of the hero that Tolkien may be most original, for all the traditional history at his command.

First, history itself. It is not only dual in its nature, one of destruction and fulfillment. The whole past of Middle-earth is the story of a continuous decline from greatness, a decline which finds its analogy in the Fall of Adam and Eve. It is the story, also, of repetition, of history repeating itself and demanding the same moral decisions age after age. It is no accident that Tolkien locates the events of *The Lord of the Rings* in a period of transition between ages when the inevitable conflicts test the moral nature of men—and hobbits. The myth man makes is the story of how he has used his imagination age after age, at moments of crisis. For history demands choice, making decisions which affect the lives of the future upon which past historical events inexorably weigh. Thus Beowulf must fight the dragon which comes uninvited into his life, if he is to assert his freedom from debilitating fear. Living beings in each age must make choices, and in fantasy the nature of these choices—or, perhaps, this Choice—is always the same, since it demands the exercise

95

of judgment which is a test of what is worth preserving in life.

History is inexorably winding down toward some unknown end, probably chaos. Created beings of the Third Age, in which the War of the Ring is fought, are less powerful because farther from the origins of their race and power than their mythic ancestors who were the first to engage in the conflicts between Good and Evil which are the stepping-stones of history. In an appendix to the third volume of *The Lord of the Rings*, Tolkien gives us an important history of the settling of Middle-earth by nearly godlike beings, the ancestors of the elves, or Eldar; and the ancestors of men (Edain). These are mythic beings who, like Adam and Eve in Christian mythology, are more than mortal and must make choices which decrease or limit their "immortal" natures. For instance, the leader of the Eldar is Fëanor, "the greatest of the Eldar in arts and lore," who comes to Middle-earth from "the Blessed Realm" in pursuit of Morgoth the Enemy, who stole the jewels called the Silmarilli. The jewels had been filled with the light from two trees, Telperion and Laurelin, "that gave light to the land of the Valar." Morgoth destroys the trees of light and steals the jewels, thereby identifying himself as a type of Satan, the Prince of Darkness who perverts or destroys the good in Nature. His theft and act of destruction initiate the conflict between good and evil which is perpetuated in the history of Middle-earth, an act of "possessiveness" Tolkien deplores. In another sense, though, Fëanor's act of placing the light in the jewels he makes as the Artist or "Jewel-smith" was the first such act; Fëanor is described as proud and "self-willed." His creation exemplifies the paradox of creative power which is also destructive, and the association of his skill in art and lore with overweening pride is typical of Tolkien's use of analogous Christian myth and his view of history as essentially moral in that it is not only a movement through time. It is also caused by the "primal desires" of created beings. Fëanor takes his people to Middle-earth in pursuit of the jewels, and in wars against Morgoth he is defeated. The race of Men, the Edain, siding with the Eldar against Morgoth, and marrying with them in the first age on Middle-earth, begin the generations of men and elven-kind about whose descendants we read in *The Lord of the Rings*. Finally, after several generations, two descendants of these first beings overthrow the Enemy, and capture one of the *silmaril* from Morgoth's crown. The other jewels are lost, and, alas, "no likeness remained in Middle-earth of Laurelin the Golden."

Tolkien has taken archetypal images of trees and jewels, light and darkness, heroic warrior and malevolent enemy, and placed them in a time out of history when Nature was more than we know it to be now, when it glowed with light of the spirit, unfallen, heavenly. We thus have a "history" which is similar to that in our familiar catalogue of myths, and yet demands that our imagination and our sense of great deeds done in civilization's infant past award belief to this mythic history of Middle-earth, which is both like and unlike what we have always believed. Fëanor is the first of the superhuman heroes to descend from the Blessed Realm to save the light, and, though defeated, he leaves heirs who must continue the struggle; Morgoth can never be finally destroyed, but will spring up again in another dark form. The struggle for power is cast in terms of an original battle at the beginning of history between super-beings who establish history as a moral progression, and who set a pattern which repeats itself over and over. The battles recur down the ages, to be fought within men as well as in the open field. Behind Tolkien's sense of history lies the principle of historical determinism, as it does in *Beowulf*, giving meaning to an individual's actions in a context larger than himself. But the basic Christian theme of free will and responsibility for one's choice means that individual beings contribute what they are.

Pride becomes the destructive characteristic of the men of Middle-earth. In the Second Age, following the defeat of Morgoth, men were given the realm of Numenor to live in, and they became the "Numenoreans," the ancestors of the ruling class of Gondor who defend Minas Tirith against Morgoth's successor in evil, Sauron. The Numenoreans, like many legendary peoples, were said to be larger in mind and body, greater in spirit, than their descendants. The beginning of civilization demands founders grand enough to fight the giants in the earth and the forces of darkness. To take but one parallel: legend has it that Britain was first settled by refugees from Troy who found giants on the island, the remains of an uncivilized past (as giants always are in myth and fairystory), who must be destroyed, just as the civilizer, Hercules, kills the giant, Anteus. And just as Adam and Eve, more beautiful and stronger than their descendants, fell from Paradise into the mortal world we now know, through pride, the Numenoreans try to be more than they are, repeating the "self-will" of their ancestors. Thus, they became greedy for wealth and power; they complained against the fate that made them mortal; and they listened to the evil advice of Sauron, who replaced Morgoth as the evil genius of the time. As their wealth and power increased, generation by generation they moved away from the original elven world spirit, and finally their king, Ar-Pharazon the Golden, became "the proudest and most powerful of all Kings, and no less than the kingship of the world was his desire." He finally attempted to conquer heaven itself, the immortal lands, and the Numenoreans were destroyed; the sea swallowed them up, much as Atlantis was lost. In this way, "the Undying Lands were removed for ever from the circles of the world. So ended the glory of Numenor" (III, 392). Only a few of the "Faithful" escaped, like Noah from the Flood, and founded the Numenorean realms in Exile, Arnor and Gondor, where we meet them in *The Lord of the Rings*, the former a nearly-forgotten memory, and the other decadent and nearly helpless before the might of a reconstituted Sauron in the Third Age. Vast areas of the former kingdoms are populated either by the tag-ends of men and dwarves or strange creatures entering upon their decline, such as the ents (who are becoming increasingly "entish", more like the trees they guard); wild Nature attacks the hobbits in the Old Forest or shelters wolves in Mirkwood. Here and there are pockets of resistance to time: the home of Elrond in Rivendell; the hidden kingdom of the elves in the beneficent forest of Lothlorien; the forgotten pocket of the Shire in which the hobbits, until now ignored by history, have hidden away. But everywhere in this ancient land are the marks of the interaction of time and created beings, now to engage in conflict once more at the end of the Third Age.

It is with no mere pedant's purpose that Tolkien includes appendices to *The Lord of the Rings* giving the history and lineage of the dominant races left on Middle-earth. History repeats itself; the struggle with Sauron has been repeated over and over in the past, and will undoubtedly recur in the future. And created beings must struggle with the Enemy. This fact makes "The Shadow of the Past" perhaps the most important single chapter in the Trilogy, because Frodo must deal with this Shadow. As we have seen, the One Ring beautifully exemplifies this fate. Frodo is simply taking up the task where others failed. Thus Isildur in an ancient battle "cut the Ring from Sauron's hand and took it for his own. Then Sauron was vanquished. . . ." But Isildur was himself slain shortly thereafter by orcs, and the Ring slipped from his finger into the river to be found by the Gollum in later days. This Ring is at one point called "Isildur's Bane," that is, his "destruction," because in his pride it destroyed him. But Frodo the Hobbit must now see how the challenge of power is to be met in his turn. And part of the irony of history lies in this repetition which demands new kinds of heroism, as well as the traditional forms, to defeat *and* fulfill time's purposes.

For there is still left in Middle-earth a fascinating variety of created beings who play parts in the War of the Ring. Sauron would like to reduce this variety of life to the slavery of uniformity, like any possessive tyrant.

> Three Rings for the Elven-kings under the sky,
>   Seven for the Dwarf-lords in their halls of
>   stone,
> Nine for Mortal Men doomed to die,
>   One for the Dark Lord on his dark throne
> In the Land of Mordor where the Shadows lie.
>   One Ring to rule them all, One Ring to find
>   them,

> One Ring to bring them all and in the
> darkness bind them
> In the Land of Mordor where the Shadows lie.

This is the rhyme, part of which is inscribed on the One Ring in Frodo's possession, that Gandalf remembers from his study of ancient lore. Its theme is the paradox of creativity in the mortal world, for the Rings made for each of the races named—elves, dwarves and "mortal men"—will be used to "bind" them so long as the Dark Lord controls the One Ring. This is perhaps the paradox of creation itself: our very existence binds us to the struggle for power in Time. But the rhyme also suggests that we must examine Tolkien's characters in terms of their relationship to power and to history. We must note the complexity of characterization accomplished by a range of diverse figures—elves, men, hobbits, wizards, and the rest—rather than by a study in depth of any one character. The imagination conceives of many kinds of living things, and it is this power that makes decisions at the crossroads of history so important. And we can see in *The Hobbit* how Tolkien's successful fusion of traditional figures like dwarves and goblins, with creatures of his own imagination, like hobbits, provided him with a *creative* history from which *The Lord of the Rings* naturally grew.

In part, this means that for Tolkien heroism is not only the traditional vision of romance: the knight in armor. Instead, in a world in transition and much like our own, another kind of hero is needed, whose triumph over the Great Enemy is both unexpected and inevitable. In an age when traditional dogmas and the inspiriting beliefs of the past are suspect or held to be irrelevant, it may be that life itself will produce an unexpected figure to undertake the Quest to redeem his fellow beings. Hence, the hobbit, who has not only wandered in the backwaters of history unacknowledged, but also is a clear case of imaginative sub-creation without the burdensome antecedents of the traditional creatures of lore. Hobbits are unknown to that living record of history, the ent Treebeard, who can not place them on the list of Living Creatures, until Pippin suggests he make a "new line":

> *Half-grown hobbits, the hole-dwellers.*
> "Put us in amongst the four, next to Man (the Big People) and you've got it" (II, 85).

The paradoxical character of fantastic reality demands hobbits, in part because the other created beings cannot fight Sauron as they can; and in part because their point of view provides Tolkien with the unique vision necessary to his history. It is from the curious, naive and relatively powerless point of view of the questing hobbits that we are shown the world of Middle-earth. They are just enough like our expectations and just enough different from them to surprise us as creatures of "imagined wonder." They are Tolkien's greatest success as a sub-creator.

Although we can appreciate the hobbits' values and admire the heroism they are capable of, they are pointedly unlike us. They are not magical creatures, nor do they use magic; they are not interested in the power over others or over Nature which magic gives. We could almost say they are not interested in power at all, and in the little of their story that we know, they have stayed out of the wars, conquests and struggles of history, as though purposefully kept back for their crucial role in the War of the Ring. They are designed to surprise us; they surprise themselves, as men often do, and *grow*. Hobbits are physically small ("ranging between two and four feet of our measure"), eat a good deal and grow rather round; they do not wear shoes because they have tough soles and thick, curly hair on their feet. They live in tunnels, or tunnel-like homes called *smials* built for large families: "Sometimes, as in the case of the Tooks of Great Smials, or the Brandybucks of Brandy Hall, many generations of relatives lived in (comparative) peace together in one ancestral and many-tunnelled mansion" (I, 27). The hobbits are very clannish, and keep long genealogies. This concern for family ties goes along with another element productive of an essential conservatism in their natures, their rural economy. "Growing food and eating it occupied most of their time." The countryside of the Shire where the hobbits live is one of farmland or pasture, much like rural England, with a bit of wildwood left here and there; it is a small world with "less noise and more green" in which self-contained and self-contented beings have settled down. In their tunnel-like homes and their economy, the hobbits are identified with a gentle, cultured Nature which is usually kindly and productive when treated with respect.

The hobbits rely on country crafts and farming; they do not have machines or factories to destroy the earth and pollute the air. Instead they live in happy, business-like conjunction with Nature; in *The Lord of the Rings*, perhaps Sam's greatest sorrow is the willful cutting-down of the avenue of chestnut trees at Bag End and the placement there of a "new mill in all its frowning and dirty ugliness: a great brick building straddling the stream, which it fouled with a steaming and stinking outflow. All along the Bywater Road every tree had been felled" (III, 365–6). Sam is a gardener by trade and inheritance; he returns as a kind of Johnny Appleseed to the Shire, and with the pollen given him by Galadriel, he makes the land grow again after the short destructive rule of the debased wizard, Saruman. The Shire is not only a gentle parody of the Garden of Eden in which Adam and Eve were placed "to dress it and to keep it," but Tolkien's retrospective vision of the countryside of England when mills had not yet fouled its fields and streams, and chestnuts still grew along the Bywater Road. For the hobbits are not only conservative in their family ties; they also represent a pastoral vision which identifies mills and machines with the earth's destruction. A well-ordered and well-farmed countryside was their favourite haunt" (I,19). A regret for past simplicity (that perhaps never actually existed) runs through Tolkien's descriptions of the Shire.

The hobbits are thus a bit like fairy-story animals, just small and hairy and funny enough to appear "quaint," and so exactly what one might expect from a whimsical English humorist. Gentle, not very serious, good fun. But hobbits must be taken more seriously than we might expect. They are enough like human beings to provide a serious commentary on our own self-satisfied conservatism. Hobbits are "as a rule, good-natured rather than beautiful, broad, bright-eyed, red-cheeked, with mouths apt to laughter, and to eating and drinking" (I, 20). They have discovered tobacco. They love giving and attending parties; significantly both *The Hobbit* and *The Lord of the Rings* open with parties that link the two books. The first party is unexpectedly forced on Bilbo by Gandalf and the dwarves, and marks the breakup of his customary, uneventful life. The second celebrates Bilbo's birthday long after his return from the Quest; it is then that Frodo replaces Bilbo as Ringbearer. This link between the generations is thus marked by a ceremony traditional in literature: the feast of friends or family which often covers up strife and disruption under the table.

The picture thus far is of a simple, familial society, not too sophisticated or self-conscious and so conforming to the pastoral society of a nursery-world. Hobbit conservatism is reflected in their government, which is minimal. There is a "Thain" and the Mayor of the chief village, and a rudimentary border patrol called the "Bounders," but the basic hobbit community is self-governing; its members obey what few general laws they have "of free will, because they were The Rules (as they said), both ancient and just." This is government by tradition, the unwritten laws of a law-abiding people handed down from generation to generation, reflecting the essential stability of the society, and not much thought about by its members. In fact, a schoolboy's conventional view of the part played by tradition and a natural respect for law and order in English society. Under this system of regulation through tradition and family training, power is rarely an issue. There is a certain class hierarchy, with wealth and family putting such families as the Baggins and the Tooks "on top," but nothing with serious political implications.

History is mostly genealogy. The hobbit museums (or Mathom-houses) exhibit remnants from the past, not because anyone cares but because hobbits cannot bear to throw anything away. Their books, in turn—and this is important—are equally unimaginative. The works they read must be "filled with things that they already knew, set out fair and square with no contradiction" (I, 28). It is only with the passing of the Third Age and the War of the Ring that the hobbits begin to think of themselves as participants in the larger sweep of history and to write histories of their part in it. While hobbits had lived in the Shire for over a millenium, they had remained isolated there, self-contained and not interested in the outside world; they had no reason to be self-conscious about time:

> there in that pleasant corner of the world they plied their well-ordered business of living, and they heeded less and less the world outside where dark things moved, until they came to think that peace and plenty were the rule in Middle-earth and the right of all sensible folk (I, 24).

The hobbits are a people without great passions or powerful ambitions, and their consequent lack of an exciting history is symptomatic. Not only are their lives simple and rather thoughtless; they are unadorned. Tolkien makes no mention of any art in hobbit houses, nor of music or poetry; hobbits probably see poetry as not suitable for the serious-minded and businesslike. This is a vital element in Tolkien's description because when history—in the guise of the dwarves journeying to revenge their race on Smaug the Dragon—knocks at Bilbo's door, that hobbit, of all his race, begins to respond to the imaginative value—and threat—of poetry. Gandalf the Wizard arranged that this unexpected visit take place, and while the dwarves eat up Bilbo's food and drink his ale and coffee, they sing. One song describes the beauty of the treasure they wish to recover; the might of the dragon guarding the gold; the dangers of the journey they are about to undertake:

The dwarves of yore made mighty spells,
While hammers fell like ringing bells
In places deep, where dark things sleep,
In hollow halls beneath the fells.

For ancient king and elvish lord
There many a gleaming golden hoard
They shaped and wrought, and light they caught
To hide in gems on hilt of sword.

Far over the misty mountains cold
To dungeons deep and caverns old
We must away ere break of day
To seek the pale enchanted gold.

(The Hobbit, 27)

The song is a poetic history of the dwarves as artisans fashioning beautiful things and of their flight from the invading dragon Smaug. The song shakes Bilbo out of his hobbit-ness, and awakens his imagination to larger things:

> As they sang the hobbit felt the love of beautiful things made by hands and by cunning and by magic moving through him, a fierce and jealous love, the desire of the hearts of dwarves. Then something Tookish woke up inside him, and he wished to go and see the great mountains, and hear the pine-trees and the waterfalls . . . *(The Hobbit, 28)*.

(Bilbo's mother had been a Took, a hobbit family thought to have elvish blood and therefore more prone to fantasy than others: hence, "Tookish.") Here are the "primal desires" and the works of the imagination the hobbit had not known in his own enclosed world; the song arouses an interest in Bilbo in "realizing imagined wonder," in perhaps coming to grips with the dragon under the Lonely Mountain. Bilbo in his own story and the hobbits in *The Lord of the Rings* are evidence of the ability of created beings to "come alive" and grow to meet the challenge which history imposes. On their respective Quests they will illustrate endurance and courage unguessed at back in the quiet Shire:

> . . . ease and peace had left this people still curiously tough. They were, if it came to it, difficult to daunt or to kill; and they were, perhaps, so unwearyingly fond of good things not least because they could, when put to it, do without them, and could survive rough handling by grief, foe, or weather in a way that astonished those who did not know them well and looked no further than their bellies and their well-fed faces (I, 25).

The hobbit, like other created things, is "in disguise," and like the typical hero of romance, it is his unexpected call to perform heroically that brings out his best.

And so in Bilbo's journey with the dwarves, which he is asked to join exactly because he is the wrong hero. Gandalf explains to the dwarves that he has introduced them to this hobbit because a new approach to dragons is needed. A direct attack on the dragon would not work without

> "a mighty Warrior, even a Hero. I tried to find one; but warriors are busy fighting one another in distant lands, and in this neighborhood heroes are scarce, or simply not to be found. Swords in these parts are mostly blunt, and axes are used for trees, and shields as cradles or dish-covers; and dragons are comfortably far-off (and therefore legendary)" (*The Hobbit*, 33–4).

After reducing history to a question of kitchen utility, Gandalf announces that the *other side* of heroism, burglary, is needed, ". . . especially when I remembered the existence of a Side-door [into the Lonely Mountain]. And here is our little Bilbo Baggins, *the* burglar, the chosen and selected burglar." Tolkien's whimsy should not disguise the importance of a definition of heroism calling for stealth, endurance, cunning, courage—all qualities Bilbo finds he possesses when he accepts the challenge and "Tookishly determined to go on with things." This backhanded approach to heroism seems a bit specious until we realize that Bilbo's experience is the prototype of Frodo's in the far more serious successor to *The Hobbit*. Frodo, too, feels himself unworthy to the great task; he does not volunteer. And while he is not moved by Bilbo's fanciful reasons but by a more serious concern, he is still the "burglar," who steals into Sauron's backdoor while the Dark Lord guards the front. Like Bilbo, Frodo succeeds in his quest because he is a hobbit: unknown, unexpected, surprisingly courageous and perservering.

Tolkien depicts both hobbits "growing up" to their respective tasks through their imaginative grasp of the challenges. We see this in Bilbo's response to song: the development of his own sub-creative ability. We have seen his response to the dark tunnels under the mountains where he finds the One Ring. There Tolkien shows that a quick wit and a passion for self-preservation have taken the place of the stolid, self-confident dependence on a good sword-arm of the romance. In the dark Bilbo runs into the Gollum, the most recent possessor of the One Ring, who threatens to catch and eat him. They agree to a riddle game: three riddles apiece, and if Bilbo can guess the riddles asked him, Gollum will lead him out from underground. The riddles are the nursery-rhymes of childhood, but they have their mythical source in the religious past of magical incantations and the secret name of God:

> Thirty white horses on a red hill,
>> First they champ,
>> Then they stamp,
> Then they stand still.   (*The Hobbit*, 81)

(Gollum wins this round by guessing, properly, "teeth.") Finally, Bilbo, who has the Ring of Power hidden in his pocket, a bit unfairly, asks Gollum to guess what is hidden there. He can't, of course, and pursues Bilbo down the tunnels until the hobbit accidently puts on the Ring, becomes invisible, and escapes back to his comrades—

through chance, granted, but also through his own quickness of wit.

Later in the journey, when the dwarves are caught in spiderwebs and Bilbo helps them escape, he makes up a tricky, utilitarian sort of rhyme to lead the spiders astray:

> Old fat spider spinning in a tree!
> Old fat spider can't see me!
>   Attercop! Attercop!
>   Won't you stop,
> Stop your spinning and look at me! (*Hobbit*, 157).

As Tolkien says, "Not very good perhaps, but then you must remember that he had to make it up himself, on the spur of a very awkward moment. It did what he wanted any way." Bilbo's increasing ability to act in the outer world beyond the safe Shire is illustrated in his handling of Gollum, the spiders, the elves who capture the travelers for a time, in his recognition of the prophecy's fulfillment which alerts the treasure-hunters to the secret door in the side of the Lonely Mountain. It is Bilbo, with his quick hobbit eye, who catches the right moment as the sun sets, not the anxious dwarves. And it is Bilbo who goes to look on the dragon sleeping in the mountain's depths; creeping down the tunnel toward the treasure room and its hideous guardian, Bilbo sees the light of the dragon's fires, hears "the unmistakable gurgling noise" of the dragon snoring in its sleep.

> It was at this point that Bilbo stopped. Going on from there was the bravest thing he ever did. The tremendous things that happened afterwards were as nothing compared to it (*Hobbit*, 204).

The small being who cannot wield a great sword can accomplish what larger heroes cannot, especially if he has the basic courage, here a kind of desperate endurance, not commitment to any particular faith in some ultimate truth. The challenge of the adventure evokes a corresponding bravery, trickiness, and imagination on the hobbit's part. Bilbo is less the romance warrior, for all his sword and little mail shirt, than the trickster who brings down the high and mighty because he is small and clever and unexpected. Of course, one of the elemental fantasies of our literature is the paradoxical triumph of the weak over the powerful: the little tailor wins a princess by killing the giant.

Bilbo illustrates not only this unexpected manipulation of power by a hobbit; he also "grows" to meet the challenges of the Quest, so that a correlation can be made between his increased power over the world and his ability to make a Secondary World of his own, through song. On his return to the Shire, Bilbo sings:

> Roads go ever ever on,
>   Over rock and under tree,
> By caves where never sun has shone,
>   By streams that never find the sea;
> Over snow by winter sown,
>   And through the merry flowers of June,
> Over grass and over stone,
>   And under mountains in the moon . . .
>   (*Hobbit*, 283).

And Gandalf is surprised. " 'My dear Bilbo!' he said. 'Something is the matter with you! You are not the hobbit that you were.' " And indeed, on his return from his adventures he is looked on as "queer," "no longer quite respectable" by the hobbits of the Shire. And in *The Lord of the Rings*, when the main action has been taken over by his nephew, and Bilbo retires to await the outcome of the War of the Rings in Rivendell, he not only writes the history of his life, but makes up elegaic verse in the manner of the elves, verse expressing the dark, dream side of the past which he, the aged hobbit, has had a part in. His "hero" is the mythical Earendil whose fate was to become a star, immortal and distant from earth, yet a guide and omen for mariners:

> And over Middle-earth he passed

and heard at last the weeping sore
of women and of elven-maids
In Elder Days, in years of yore.
But on him mighty doom was laid,
till Moon should fade, an orbed star
to pass, and tarry never more
on Hither Shores where mortals are;
or ever still a herald on
an errand that should never rest
to bear his shining lamp afar,
the Flammifer of Westernesse (I, 311).

The chant suggests sadness, regret, for the being rendered immortal by being set apart from others in the heavens, and is a perfect complement to the Council of Elrond, where Bilbo sings this composition one evening, for it reminds us of the doom imposed by time upon the elves and the others present; and of the transmutation of adventures and created beings into legends. Those who are rigid in vision and not imaginative, who are limited by the possessiveness of the self, like the Gollum or the trolls symbolically turned to stone by Gandalf's magic in *The Hobbit*, can have no poetic sense of life. Consequently they are afraid of death and cannot use fantasy, in Tolkien's sense, to understand it.

Indeed, the old hobbit can be not only elegaic but prophetic, and at the Council of Elrond, answers the skeptic, Boromir, who questions that Frodo's ring is the Ring of Power, with a prophetic rhyme:

All that is gold does not glitter,
  Not all those who wander are lost;
The old that is strong does not wither,
  Deep roots are not reached by the frost.
From the ashes a fire shall be woken,
  A light from the shadows shall spring;
Renewed shall be blade that was broken:
  The crownless again shall be king (I, 325).

The past comes to the aid of the present, imaginative intuition to the council of those in despair. For Bilbo

110

to have moved from an ordinary hobbit to a mystic seer living among the elves in Rivendell suggests something about the nature of time: for Bilbo has lived beyond his normal years (though hobbits are long-lived), and he will ultimately be granted immortality, like the elves and the hero, Eärendil. But for the moment of the War he remains in Middle-earth to turn history into legend, and to read myth in history, both means of transforming time into eternity. And in his prophetic rhyme, an echo of the riddle contest with the Gollum, he speaks of the past and future from a position above history, looking down on it as events move inexorably toward their conclusion and the end of the Third Age.

And here is another of the ironies with which Tolkien enriches his history: it is only the passage through life—with its dark trials, with the necessary immersion in the temporal world—that enables us to transcend this world. The hobbit who remains at home thinks only of silver teaspoons, like Lobelia Sackville-Baggins. But the journeys Bilbo and Frodo make "stretch" them into other beings with a life beyond the world of time and journeys. Bilbo's imagination stretches too, and, like the legends he celebrates in his poetry, Bilbo becomes legendary himself.

The wisdom which the hobbit-hero traditionally brings back to his people does not come into its own until the Ring passes to Bilbo's nephew and heir, Frodo. But Bilbo's journey prepares for the more historically important one; and his transcendence of time and departure from Middle-earth at the trilogy's close is a paradoxical affirmation of our own mortality. And finally, we cannot forget the importance of "grace" or forgiveness and pity which the hobbits show toward the Gollum. Both Bilbo and Frodo can forgive his wretched desire for the Ring, a desire they share, and if the hobbits were human, we would have to speak of their "humanity" which becomes, as we shall see, the expression of the imagination in fellow-feeling.

The hobbit provides Tolkien with an important point of view, a vision of reality by which other characters and events may be evaluated. This is one role played by the hobbits who accompany Frodo on his Quest: Sam the

111

gardener's son, Merry and Pippin. Together they form a feudal band like that in *Beowulf*, the hero's loyal followers who march "Erect like guards, like sentinels, as though ready/To fight" (ll.305–6). They help Frodo escape from the pursuing Black Riders, and insist on accompanying him on the journey south toward Mordor. Their loyalty to the Ring-bearer is unquestioning, an example of brotherly love which finds its epitome in Sam who goes into Mordor itself. Pippin and Merry split off with the other Allies and become knights in the armed forces of Rohan and Gondor; Pippin is even knighted by Denethor the High Steward of Gondor, in a ceremony which is meaningful exactly because he is a small hobbit who could never occupy the place of a full-sized warrior in the battalions ranged against Sauron, but who is to be respected for his courage and the loyalty he can offer. And Denethor promises to return the deserved rewards to his new ally: "fealty with love, valour with honour, oath-breaking with vengeance" (III, 31). Merry, who serves as a similar knight-mascot in the army of Rohan, has the honor of bringing down the sinister Nazgûl lord himself. Useless for the great battles, he is present when the Nazgûl attacks Eowyn, the "Valkyrie" of the story, and with his small but efficient sword cuts the sinews of the evil being's leg so that Eowyn may finish the creature off. The ancient sword had been taken from the treasure-trove of the Barrow-downs back at the Quest's beginning; its purpose was only to fight against the forces of darkness, and with the blow fatal to the Nazgûl, it "burns up." "No other blade, not though mightier hands had wielded it, would have dealt that foe a wound so bitter, cleaving the flesh, breaking the spell that knit his unseen sinews to his will" (III,146). The small hobbit came along at the right moment in history for his task. And like the Nazgûl, he too has a "will" which drives him forward. All the hobbits on the Quest share the will to endure in the face of great odds, and hobbit perseverance becomes an asset even for men. Tolkien never betrays our trust in hobbits, although he comes close when they appear "quaint" or "whimsical." He gives them a moral stature which takes them from parody into true heroism.

And this, finally, is the significance of seeing the world of Middle-earth from the hobbit point of view. Although the varied and often alien life outside the Shire is new to them, the hobbits help to make the Quest into a moral history—through their comments, through their decisions, most of all through their growing sense of moral responsibility. We see Bilbo in *The Hobbit* take up the Arkenstone, which Thorin seeks above all the treasure in Smaug's cave, and use it to force the leader of the dwarves to divide his recovered wealth with the other beings who have suffered from the depradations of Smaug. We do not see much of Bilbo's decision-making here; it simply happens, and Thorin is forced to give in. But it represents the growth of the hobbit's sense of moral responsibility for others which the possessive dwarves do not feel. And we find this awakening, this decision-making, extended in Frodo's case where, time after time, he must determine to carry the Ring of Power forward to its destruction. As we shall see, the hobbits provide the basic moral commentary in *The Lord of the Rings* because their history, their natures as hobbits, makes them more available to "realize imagined wonder" than other creatures. As they develop in the journey outside the Shire, they illustrate the respect for other living things which we have called "humanity" and which is available only to the flexible, those with imagination.

Chapter Four: Elves, Dwarves, Wizards

The hobbits are unique creations who take on some
of the virtuous characteristics of men without being men.
The elves and the dwarves, on the other hand, depend
for their imaginative effect upon Tolkien's modification of
the long fairy-story tradition they represent. Both races
are less important for their activity in the Quest or in the
War of the Ring than for their places in the declining
history of Middle-earth. They stand for a certain relationship to time and to Nature which is valuable and yet not
as effective as that of the hobbits or of men in the transitional end of the Third Age. In *The Lord of the Rings*, the
elves and dwarves stand in the background, symboli-

figures who address our imaginations from the fairy-story past and are not involved in the great moral choices Frodo must make. Their time for shaping the world is over. The elves, especially, are relics: closer to the origins of life than living men, those left in Middle-earth possess immortality, by their choice, but, like the dwarves dispossessed of their halls under the Lonely Mountain or in the mines of Moria, they are "exiles" from the Blessed Realm. And with the end of the Third Age, even though the Allies triumph over Sauron, the elves must leave their homes in Middle-earth and "pass into the Uttermost West." Those who choose to remain in this world become mortal and die in Middle-earth.

Consequently, as Tolkien suggests, for the elves "all chances of the War of the Ring were fraught with sorrow" (III, 389). The elves have kept three of the Rings they made, but since the ultimate control of the Rings lies with Sauron, they are potentially under his command. As Elrond explains, the three elven Rings "were not made as weapons of war or conquest; that is not their power.

> Those who made them did not desire strength or domination or hoarded wealth, but understanding, making and healing, to preserve all things unstained. These things the Elves of Middle-earth have in some measure gained, bought with sorrow. But all that has been wrought by those who wield the Three will turn to their undoing, and their minds and hearts will become revealed to Sauron, if he regains the One" (I, 352).

Sauron "ensnared" the elven-smiths who made the rings through their interest in gaining knowledge; the Ring has power over the desire for whatever is deemed most powerful by a particular race or person. The elves had hoped that with the Rings they could "heal the hurts of the world." But in a world like ours, even motives like this can be perverted. Further, fate has determined that even should the dangerous Ring of Power be destroyed, the Three Rings that remain to the elves "will fail, and many fair things will fade and be forgotten." As Galadriel tells Frodo,

> ". . . if you succeed, then our power is diminished, and Lothlorien will fade, and the tides of Time will sweep it away. We must depart into the West, or dwindle to a rustic folk of dell and cave, slowly to forget and to be forgotten" (I, 472).

Here is one of the moments when Tolkien fuses the Secondary World of the Rings' history with the Primary World of his readers. For the Ring *is* destroyed, and elves have indeed "dwindled" to the mysterious winged "little people" of the fairy-stories. Galadriel evidently prophesied rightly. Thus in *The Lord of the Rings* the elves who remain in Middle-earth represent the pathos of a dying culture passing into history as it finds itself out of step with the changing world. Their songs are of the past, of the absent, of beauty departed:

> Snow-white! Snow-white! O Lady clear!
>   O Queen beyond the Western Seas!
> O Light to us that wander here
>   Amid the world of woven trees!
>   * * *
> O Elbereth! Gilthoniel!
>   We still remember, we who dwell
> In this far land beneath the trees,
>   Thy starlight on the Western Seas (I,117).

The elves' past is heavily sentimentalized, as the ballad of Amroth and Nimrodel, mythic elvish lovers, indicates; and this is in keeping with the role the elves play in the larger struggle against Sauron.

For the elves' kind of power cannot now be effective against the Dark Lord. Their elegiac songs and pastoral lives in the trees of Lothlorien and the secure bowers of Rivendell are symptomatic of their essentially conservative position; they may preserve and guide, but to join in the wars is to destructively seek power. Thus Elrond, the aged

116

prince of the elves, is described in conventional terms. His face is "neither old nor young, though in it was written the memory of many things both glad and sorrowful . . . his eyes were grey as a clear evening, and in them was a light like the light of stars. Venerable he seemed as a king crowned with many winters . . ." (I, 299). Elrond lives in both worlds, Middle-earth and the Blessed Realm of the Immortals; his power is that of a superior, perhaps divine, being, but his suffering, his part in the past wars, has given him the knowledge to heal, to understand, a knowledge gained no other way. He is the archetypal king of a dying land and the convention of his physical description is not an imaginative failure on Tolkien's part. This is Frodo's view of him, telling us something about Frodo and his discovery of the greatness of the past. And Frodo's response to Elrond is ours, also, a response evoked by the formula used in tales of the imagination age after age to describe the wise Ruler.

But the War of the Ring will bring the Third Age to an end, and Elrond will leave Middle-earth. This note of inevitable pathos is part of Tolkien's sense of the past, for the beautiful things in life will finally be destroyed. Elrond's daughter, the lovely princess Arwen Undomiel, will choose to marry the mortal Aragorn and at last die alone in Cerin Amroth after the elves have departed. And although Elrond is powerful enough in Middle-earth to control the Loudwater, sending a flood down against the Ringwraiths pursuing Frodo, his real power is conservative; it is in Rivendell that the Great Council is held, one of many such councils in *The Lord of the Rings* when the good and the beautiful debate together in a civilized formality about controlling chaos. This combination of pathos and civility in the elves appears most significantly in Galadriel, the elven queen living with her people in the depths of Lothlorien. She too is a council-holder, having first called the White Council which had considered the spreading might of Sauron. And the effort of her ancient wisdom (like Elrond she is both wise and beautiful, the body showing forth the spirit) is to counsel and to preserve. Thus the Ring-bearers wander in the tree-city of Caras Galadon, and see Galadriel and her consort, Celeborn, walking among the trees. They have "no sign of age . . . upon them, unless it were in the depths of their eyes; for these were keen as lances in the starlight, and yet profound, the wells of deep memory" (I, 459). Like the lost Garden of Eden in which, too, the plants and flowers were intensely colored and scented, the world of the elves is essentially conservative; its inhabitants seek to postpone the inevitable destruction of "many fair things." In turn, Galadriel's "counseling" is to show each being who appears before her his true self, and to ask moral choices of him. She makes each feel "that he was offered a choice between a shadow full of fear that lay ahead, and something that he greatly desired: clear before his mind it lay, and to get it he had only to turn aside from the road and leave the Quest and the war against Sauron to others" (I, 463). Galadriel is not the conventional temptress, a siren encouraging the Company to leave its duty; as Aragorn says, "There is in her and in this land no evil, unless a man bring it hither himself. Then let him beware!" Her long, steady look is a test of the capacity for fortitude and endurance on the part of the Fellowship. Significantly, Boromir questions her goodness; it is he who later is the only member of the Company to break his "oath" of loyalty. No man knows what is in him until the test comes. She shows Sam and Frodo in the basin of water, the Mirror of Galadriel, what events or scenes they wish to see there: "Some never come to be unless those that behold the visions turn aside from their path to prevent them. The Mirror is dangerous as a guide of deeds" (I, 470).

Galadriel's power seems magical to the hobbits (or to us) who do not know the unseen world as the elves do. But Tolkien is careful to show us magic for its moral implications: those who use it wisely demand choice and moral decision, often from themselves. Thus Galadriel's real task, as one of the Guardians of Middle-earth, is to preserve the world of the elves from Sauron: one of the Three Rings made for the elves is hers, Nenya, the Ring of Adamant. Should Sauron gain the One Ring, then she and her people would fall to his power. Perhaps more importantly, Galadriel herself is available for either good or evil; she is not the mere image of goodness. Her mind is powerful enough to hold Sauron at bay: "I perceive the Dark Lord and know his mind, or all of his mind that concerns the Elves. And he gropes ever to see me and my thought. But still the door is closed!" (I, 472). Frodo, seeking to escape his burden, offers her the One Ring; she refuses because it would give her power to supplant Sauron, and "in place of the Dark Lord you will set up a Queen. And I shall not be dark, but beautiful and terrible as the Morning and the Night! All shall love me and despair" (I, 473). Her power would lie in sexual dominance, the power over men represented by the Beautiful Lady Without Mercy whom John Keats characterizes as "La Belle Dame sans Merci." This would be only to substitute one figure of power for another. Furthermore, to assume such power over others invites destruction of the true self. The Ring, Galadriel reminds Frodo, "gives power according to the measure of each possessor." And before using that power, "you would need to become far stronger, and to train your will to the domination of others" (I, 474). Like all beings in Middle-earth, Galadriel must make choices, too, and she chooses to remain herself and accept the fate of her nature: ". . . suddenly she laughed again, and lo! she was shrunken: a slender elf-woman, clad in simple white, whose gentle voice was soft and sad. 'I pass the test,' she said. 'I will diminish, and go into the West, and remain Galadriel!' " (I, 473–4). Although she does not participate directly in the action of the Trilogy, Galadriel represents the beauty of sacrifice for the good of the whole world community. And she is present not only as a preserver of life; she also serves as inspiration for the active defenders of Middle-earth. Her potential sexual destructiveness is transformed into inspiration. For instance, she inspires love from Gimli the Dwarf, and so contributes to the forging of bonds between two races that had been historical enemies. Meeting her for the first time, Gimli "looked suddenly into the heart of an enemy and saw there love and understanding. Wonder came into his face, and then he smiled in answer: 'Yet more fair is the living land of Lorien, and the Lady Galadriel is above all the jewels that lie beneath the earth!' " (I, 461). High praise from Gimli. Henceforth, the dwarf fights for his "Lady's" love.

Again, her gift of a vial of light to Frodo gives him courage against the huge spider, Shelob, who guards the tunnel beneath Cirith Ungol, and represents all that Galadriel is not: the destructive, selfish female who "served none but herself, drinking the blood of Elves and Men, . . . who only desired death for all others, mind and body, and for herself a glut of life, alone . . ." (II, 423). While Shelob may seem a long way from the ruler in Lorien, she is part of Tolkien's art in presenting counterparts to even the best beings in the complex web of creation, the perversions of goodness to which anyone may come who chooses the wrong path. And while Tolkien has varied his "evil" characters enormously, they all share with Shelob in the imprisoning world vision of those without imagination. Galadriel does not command; she inspires the choice of courage over cowardice, and the will in Sam to continue the battle even after Frodo has been captured by the enemy. And it is she who gives Sam the gift of pollen which, scattered over the Shire, renews and intensifies its natural life, thereby returning to Middle-earth something of that natural beauty possessed by the Garden of Eden and which Frodo finds again in the forests of Lorien. "He felt a delight in wood and the touch of it, neither as forester nor as carpenter; it was the delight of the living tree itself" (I, 455). The elves live in such trees; close to the pastoral world of Nature, they let it live for itself. They do not wish to change the world in their own image, a selfish and destructive wish. Galadriel epitomizes this generosity, and also the limitations of the elves as warriors against Sauron.

In the background of the action in *The Lord of the Rings*, Tolkien places another race traditionally important in fairy-stories. Like the elves, the dwarves are conservators, guardians of the treasures beneath the earth, but unlike the elves of the forest, they are traditionally associated with greed, the hoarding of treasure, with selfishness which can be destructive. They are represented as craftsmen who take minerals and make them into jewels, and so, by the very nature of their art, alter the shape of the earth, in contrast to the elves who live among the trees without changing their life. However, Tolkien's view of the dwarves changes from one book to the next.

In *The Hobbit*, the attempt of the dwarves under Thorin Oakenshield to regain their ancestral treasures from Smaug initiates the Quest and Bilbo's journey to the East. They also seek revenge for the past. For the dwarves history has been the accumulation of treasure which in turn awakes enemies who wish to possess it—and them. Thus in Moria the dwarves had dug for *mithril*, a precious metal, a search in the bowels of the earth which arouses the Balrog, a beast who nearly destroys Gandalf. The dwarves must flee the subterranean palace, Khazad-dûm, and again, when they have dug a new world in Erebor, the Lonely Mountain, the rumors of their treasure bring down upon them Smaug the Golden, "greatest of the dragons of his day," who destroys their kingdom, and sleeps on the hoard of gold in the Great Chamber of Thror. The pursuit of gold is natural to dwarves, but Tolkien makes a moral connection between this passion and their natural enemy, the dragon or fire-drake. The hoarding of gold inevitably invites such destruction. When Beowulf learns the fire-drake has descended upon his people, he sees it as a punishment for sin, perhaps in himself. If we think of the dragon as allegorical, drawn to treasure-hoards which he guards, thereby keeping the gold from a useful life in the human world, the connection between sin and reprisal becomes important. For the dragon is, after all, a "worm," a reptile representing the narrow, selfish life of the imprisoned soul shut in the perversely unnatural body, winged, spouting fire and smoke, a night traveler, secretive, like all evil things. And as such, it represents the perverse side of man's power, the dread of human beings made manifest so it can be dealt with, "the malice, greed, destruction" that is the evil side of even the most heroic life.[15]

The nature of Tolkien's dwarves gives their enemies a hold over them. In *The Hobbit*, after Smaug has been killed by the Men of Dale, Thorin insists on keeping the recovered treasure, and denying the right even the fire-drake's victims to share it. Bilbo feels that the claims of others to the treasure is justified, but

> he did not reckon with the power that gold has upon which a dragon has long brooded, nor with dwarvish hearts. Long hours in the past days Thorin had spent in the treasury, and the lust of it was heavy on him (*Hobbit*, 250).

The consequence of this destructive passion is a siege and a great battle and the death of Thorin Oakenshield, whose deathbed injunction is the obvious one: "If more of us valued food and cheer and song above hoarded gold, it would be a merrier world" (*Hobbit*, 273). And in the history of the dwarves appended to *The Lord of the Rings,* Tolkien notes that it is their nature which makes them vulnerable to the power of Sauron: "The only power over them that the Rings wielded was to inflame their hearts with a greed of gold and precious things, so that if they lacked them all other good things seemed profitless, and they were filled with wrath and desire for vengeance on all who deprived them" (III, 446). Their possessiveness is worked out even in their language which has changed little over the centuries. It is a language of lore, of secret knowledge which few beings beside the dwarves understand. Furthermore, dwarves have each a secret, "true" name, and another for use in the outside world, again suggestive of their secretive character.

It is significant that this picture of the dwarves is modified by Tolkien in the Trilogy. There Gimli appears as a brusque, short-tempered but not unlovable warrior who, like his ancestors, will not be "enslaved to another will" (III, 447). But his part in the development of the trilogy is minor, and the dwarvish lust for treasure has been altered for a more promising ecological and aesthetic position. Gimli describes for the elf, Legolas, the magnificent caverns he has seen in Helm's Deep, the secret retreat of the Men of Rohan in time of war, and his experience there evokes a torrent of rhetoric not to be expected from a secretive, laconic dwarf. His vision is that of the craftsman whose delight is in making things according to their nature:

> "No dwarf could be unmoved by such loveliness. None of Durin's race would mine those caves for stones or ore, not if diamonds and gold could be got there. Do you cut down groves of blossoming trees in the springtime for firewood? We would tend these glades of flowering stone, not quarry them" (II,195).

The emphasis of his speech is upon "tending" and conserving these "glades" beneath the earth which duplicate the elven forests above ground, a respect for the earth and its treasures which men in the Fourth Age must learn to show. But in *The Lord of the Rings* the dwarf represents the artist as "revealer" of hidden beauty and its caretaker and preserver. As for others, the power of the artist over his material is a precious trust.

Gimli serves another related thematic purpose. Tolkien constructs an enmity between dwarves and elves which is not traditional, but is based in part on the dwarves' mistreatment by the elf king of Mirkwood in *The Hobbit*. Gimli becomes the close companion of the elf, Legolas, who journeys with the Fellowship south, and in turn, the first dwarf in many ages permitted to enter Lorien where he meets and admires the elven queen, Galadriel. After the Third Age has ended and many of the Fellowship leave Middle-earth for the Eternal Land, Gimli is permitted to accompany them, an unheard of privilege. This friendship between dwarf and elf is part of the Trilogy's theme of love and respect shared among different beings. The supposed warfare between the two races is the failure of such respect and of their ability to put the community of being before themselves.

In the hierarchy of power in Tolkien's Middle-earth, the wizards are a separate race occupying the highest rung; they possess supernatural powers. In addition, Gandalf represents most explicitly to the other inhabitants of

Middle-earth the hidden truths of that world and the necessity of continuous moral choice. He inspires the Allies against Sauron with insight and courage, and counsels them when they must choose between good and evil. Like the other wielders of "magic," his "art" is actually not power over the phenomenal world so much as the knowledge of created beings, of history, which he uses to guide his hearers rather than to direct their wills through external control. Knowledge *is* power but it must be used with discretion. Gandalf's is an intellectual wisdom available to no other figure in *The Lord of the Rings*. While Denethor or Saruman can understand ancient lore and read cosmic purposes in the stars, only Gandalf seems uncorrupted by his power and uses it for good purposes. Since his nature is intelligence or mind, the wizard comes closest of all beings to the danger of intellectual pride, a fate which overtakes Saruman. Knowledge must be used for the good of others, to guide hobbits and men in positive actions. In this sense, Gandalf, as Tolkien describes him, is indeed an "angel" come down among men; he has the task of guiding Middle-earth for its salvation, and so like the others in the Fellowship, is a guardian, a "steward," as he calls himself. And as Gandalf is a wizard or "wise man," his knowledge of the power of words suggests that he represents something of the author, J.R.R. Tolkien, himself. Like Gandalf, Tolkien has studied the records of men left from the past, as a scholar and historian of Middle-earth. But this knowledge of "lore" can give the historian power to destroy as well as save; Saruman or even Sauron the Great is the other side of the artist who knows the power of fantasy in the real world.

Wizards are traditionally associated with magic, with control over the forces of nature exercised by calling on the spirits inhabiting that world. Often associated with alchemy, astrology, with the early sciences of the Middle Ages, and the knowledge of obscure gods or demons before that, they have been seen as outside the orthodox human community, potentially dangerous to its stability because of more than human connections. Tolkien plays with this tradition when he represents the hobbits of the

Shire treating Gandalf with caution whenever he shows up, finally appearing as a maker of fireworks for Bilbo's birthday party in order to allay their suspicions. Often the power of wizards is crudely exercised, as when the Witch of Endor calls up the spirit of the prophet Samuel to advise King Saul in the Bible (I Samuel: 28). But traditionally theirs is a more sophisticated approach to the living and the dead; their power lies in knowledge of the laws that guide Nature: how to read the stars and foretell the future, how to make fire through will and incantation; as Gandalf does. One can see how very important incantation, the ritual use of words, would be in defining the wizard's power; as metaphors, words both disguise and reveal the underlying truths upon which power is finally based.

Magic, if that term must be used here, may also be distinguished in its purpose. Black magic is power exercised over evil spirits, usually for evil purposes; there is malice involved. But white magic, or theurgy, enables the magician to control the great spirits of the universe, for good purposes: to heal the sick, redress wrongs, cleanse and improve the world. The two appear side by side in Shakespeare's play *The Tempest*. The witch Sycorax uses black magic, imprisoning Ariel in a tree and begetting a son as animal-like, as base in mind and feeling as she. Prospero, the examplar of white magic and an obvious model for Tolkien's Gandalf, has gained what appears to be supernatural power through his intelligence, which enables him to read in books the lore that controls both the spirits of the deep and Ariel, the higher spirit who works his transformations for him. This "learning" is to be used for the good of individuals and of the community in which they live: Prospero punishes and then forgives the men who took his dukedom away and set him and his daughter adrift on the sea; he betroths his daughter Miranda to a suitable prince; Ariel is freed to return to his own nature; and, finally, Prospero himself gives up his "magic" powers:

> I'll break my staff,
> Bury it certain fadoms in the earth,

125

> And deeper than did ever plummet sound
> I'll drown my book (V. i).

Like the artist, Prospero used his powers to create fantasy, images of the Secondary World, and so to challenge the rationality of men accustomed to using their reason for evil purposes. Prospero returns with his family to Milan, as an intelligent human being, no longer the magician. To have remained with this power would have made him more than human, and might have extended the temptation to control other men. Power must be defined by virtuous action, and by humane virtues of love and forgiveness. It is Gandalf who counsels Frodo to show pity and mercy to the Gollum, even though that creature is on the enemy's side. This rational and loving exercise of the imagination for the good of others distinguishes the practitioners of white magic and makes them representative of humane intelligence, like Prospero and Gandalf.

Behind this more-than-human perception lies another distinction in the cases of Gandalf and Prospero: they are aware, as others are not, of a supernatural purpose in the universe, of a moral order which directs trivial actions and seemingly unrelated events, and which can be discerned by wizards and elves, by the researchers into ancient lore. Thus in spite of his sufferings, Prospero can tell Miranda that "Providence divine" brought them safely to the island where they are now living; and Ariel tells the shipwrecked travelers that he, a spirit, is the instrument of Fate. Tolkien is following Shakespeare, then, in linking the best intelligences with the perception of cosmic and controlling realities. Gandalf is wise about the ways of hobbits, his special study; he has spent much of his time wandering Middle-earth, investigating the growing menace of Sauron as his shadow lengthens; he can speak to eagles. But he reminds us and his companions in the war against evil that there are larger purposes in the world, and that no one is insignificant or without meaning in life. Thus he describes to the bewildered Frodo the history of the Ring Bilbo had "stolen" from the Gollum and suggests that Bilbo's find was more than chance:

"Behind that there was something else at work, beyond any design of the Ring-maker. I can put it no plainer than by saying that Bilbo was *meant* to find the Ring, and *not* by its maker. In which case you also were *meant* to have it. And that may be an encouraging thought" (I, 88).

In other words, the forces for good in the universe are somehow behind the selection of Frodo as the responsible Ring-bearer. Again, it is Gandalf who suggests that pity and mercy must be shown the Gollum because he is somehow bound up with the fate of the Ring: "My heart tells me that he has some part to play yet, for good or ill, before the end; and when that comes, the pity of Bilbo may rule the fate of many—yours not least" (I, 93). Gandalf's wisdom finds expression, in part, in his humility: "For even the very wise cannot see all ends."

Finally, behind wisdom and perception lies Gandalf's real significance in the Trilogy: the connection which he represents between power and responsibility. He puts his wisdom to the service of the community of Middle-earth without being led into the sin of pride which leads other "Guardians" like Saruman and Denethor astray, into thinking they can compete with Sauron. Wisdom must be exercised in the world, and its possessor must take responsibility for its conscientious and imaginative employment among living creatures. And thus we see Gandalf rarely using "magic" save in moments of desperation. Rather, he appears more often as the Counselor who persuades others to accept their responsibilities. He appears in this guise in *The Hobbit* where he turns up Bilbo as a "burglar" for the dwarves and reveals to the expedition that a secret entrance to the Lonely Mountain exists, one Smaug does not know about. He reads the runes on a "lost" map with his handy knowledge of lore. But, although he helps the company of dwarves and Bilbo out of several scrapes, on the whole he leaves the important decisions to individuals: Bilbo must make his important decision to go down into the dragon's cavern by himself. Gandalf knows that created beings have free will which they must exercise for themselves, and he serves as a guiding "angel" only within limits.

More importantly, in *The Lord of the Rings* he serves as the wise coordinator of the war against Sauron, where we see how power must be exercised by the wise and yet controlled so that it is not self-destructive. Wizards have long been active in Middle-earth, each with a special field of study, much like a modern scholar: Radagast the Brown specializes in the lore and language of birds; Gandalf in hobbits; Saruman in the history of the Rings. But Gandalf, at least, also sees his task as a guardianship, and he guards the Shire from enemies beyond the power of hobbits to control. For this reason he disappears for long periods, seeking the Gollum, or striving to foresee Sauron's next move. Such guardianship has made "possible the long peace of the Shire." The hobbits "were, in (I, 25). He is a storehouse and interpreter of history fact, sheltered, but they had ceased to remember it" which threatens to destroy Middle-earth as the power of Sauron grows.

But his ability to read "The Shadow of the Past" and to see, as a responsible historian should, the lines of historical development gives him power over the seeming inevitability of its movement. The past can be read and its challenge accepted by those who know how to scan its pages. Gandalf knows that the Ring is inscribed with two lines of verse in Elvish letters but in the debased language of Mordor. When he learns of the Ring found again with "marks upon it that the skilled, maybe, could still see and read," he goes to Gondor where the ancient records of the kings are stored, "many records that few now can read, even of the lore-masters, for their scripts and tongues have become dark to later men." And there he reads an ancient scroll written by Isildur himself, who took the Ring from Sauron's hand, and wrote down its history. Scholarly research pays off, and when the Ring Frodo carries is cast into the fire, the ancient prophecy appears. Gandalf can then counsel Frodo about its meaning, about the Gollum, and about the hobbit's responsibility for this power he has unwittingly received. Gandalf understands the *moral* implications of history and advises Frodo not to kill the Gollum, who now suffers from his own desire for power and may, in the end, be necessary to the working out of its effects. And this, in turn, is advice which requires courage and the assumption of responsibility on Frodo's part, advice from an historian expressive of "commitment" and "relevance" that might well be considered in the Primary World of today.

Again, much of this wizard's control over the developing history of Middle-earth lies in his ability to read and use *words*. He opens the long-shut gates of Moria because he can read their secret meaning. He passes his hands over the rock, and a design appears etched on the surface, "like slender veins of silver running in the stone." Heraldic devices appear to mark the past of elves and dwarves who shared this gateway between upper and lower worlds:

> "There are the emblems of Durin!" cried
> Gimli.
> "And there is the Tree of the High Elves!"
> said Legolas.
> "And the Star of the House of Feanor," said
> Gandalf. "They are wrought of *ithildin* that
> mirrors only starlight and moonlight, and sleeps
> until it is touched by one who speaks words
> now long forgotten in Middle-earth" (I, 397).

And the doors open only when the proper word is spoken, in this case "Friend," for they are doors "governed by words," as Gandalf says. In the fairy tale, when the Queen finally learns the threatening dwarf's name is "Rumpelstiltskin" she has won the battle and saved her baby from him. In such a tale the dwarf, from the dark bowels of the earth, represents the "lower" world of uncivilized inhumanity and chaos. And it is not only a single word but the element of ritual in speaking it that expresses power. The ordering of words is an art, and argues for the power of the ordering mind which puts them together in a meaningful form. Thus the mind triumphs over chaos with its lack of "syntax," its failure of ordered meaning.

If we look closely at the "magic" in *The Lord of the Rings*, we can see that magical acts are often the powerfull use of words. Gandalf speaks the word "Friend" and the doors of Moria open. Samwise, attacking the great spider, Shelob, calls upon Galadriel far away beyond the mountains of Mordor:

> And then his tongue was loosed and his voice cried in a language which he did not know:
>
> A Elbereth Gilthoniel
> o menel palan-díriel,
> le nallon sí di'nguruthos!
> A tíro nin, Fanuilos!
>
> And with that he staggered to his feet and was Samwise the hobbit, Hamfast's son, again (II, 430).

His courage renewed, his "indomitable spirit" seems to relight the Phial of Galadriel; it blazes forth, and its light strikes "from eye to eye" in the wounded monster, driving her back. Here light, the ancient symbol of intelligence piercing the darkness of chaos, becomes an actual weapon against evil. Tolkien is careful to link these "magical" moments to the moral nature of his characters; their deathless ability to summon courage or loyalty or love in a crisis gives the ritual use of words their ultimate value. In this way wisdom lives in words themselves; Gandalf is not around when Samwise and Frodo must make decisions and invoke the aid of the past in their journey into Sauron's country.

Gandalf's strength also lies in his morality, here defined in terms of the community's needs when confronted with evil. He accepts the responsibility for other lives which his wisdom requires, to be contrasted with other wizards: Radagast the Brown, a frightened ninny who keeps out of harm's way; and Saruman, the erstwhile Head of the Order of Wizards, who becomes the pawn of Sauron because his knowledge leads to pride. Saruman wishes to gain the One Ring. He tells Gandalf that with the coming of the Age of Men, the Wise should rule: "we must have power, power to order all things as we will, for that good which only the Wise can see." He tells Gandalf that by joining with the rising might of Sauron, the Wise "may with patience come at last to direct its courses, to control it.

> We can bide our time, we can keep our thoughts in our hearts, deploring maybe evils done by the way, but approving the high and ultimate purpose: Knowledge, Rule, Order; all the things that we have so far striven in vain to accomplish. . . . There need not be, there would not be, any real change in our designs, only in our means" (I, 340).

This is, of course, to put the end before the means to it, and as Gandalf looks about him at Isengard, he sees the pits and forges, the houses for wolves and orcs which Saruman has substituted for the natural world in order to attain power. Knowledge, Rule and Order have become meaningless under such a system; intelligence has been turned to private and limited ends. The consequence is that Saruman's will is captured by the Dark Lord. Saruman fails where Gandalf succeeds; he succumbs to the lure of his own wisdom and assumes that he has enough knowledge to counter or direct forces far greater than his own, greater in part because Sauron appeals to his essential, and therefore vulnerable, being. Gandalf is always represented, on the other hand, as properly humble toward his knowledge. Often efforts against the enemy tire him, as when he stops the Balrog with a word of command, but more importantly, when he refuses the One Ring:

"With that power I should have power too great and terrible. And over me the Ring would gain a power still greater and more deadly. . . . Yet the way of the Ring to my heart is by pity, pity for weakness and the desire of strength to do good. . . . The wish to wield it would be too great for my strength" (I, 95).

This is the wisdom of practical common sense based on the thorough knowledge of the self and its limitations, even in an "angel." Even Gandalf refuses to look in the Palentir of Orthanc when it accidently comes to him; he is not ready to face Sauron in this instrument of power. Knowledge of himself and his limitations, the limitations of Knowledge, perhaps, enables him to counsel others, and to encourage them to make their own decisions. When Saruman appears, a captive to the ents, in his own tower of Orthanc, he represents barren knowledge overwhelmed by Nature; the ents have flooded his machines and wolf pits and have begun to replant the trees and gardens he had destroyed. But even in defeat the wizard uses words to try to overcome his besiegers on their own ground, so to speak; he succeeds in giving the assembled allies the impression of wisdom, kindliness, and ill-rewarded merit:

another voice spoke, low and melodious, its very sound an enchantment, . . . none were unmoved; none rejected its pleas and its commands without an effort of mind and will, so long as its master had control of it (II, 234).

Spell-bound, men believe as the immediate suggestion and the apparent truths demand. Saruman uses a voice which "*seemed* wise and reasonable," writes Tolkien, and "seems" is the crucial word about the appearances which cover the truth in Saruman's "magic," which is nothing more than what his listeners wish to hear. Significantly, Gandalf "made no sign"; he does nothing to break the spell; men must choose their own freedom. And it is the dwarf Gimli who suddenly speaks up from outside this mind-pervading voice, putting the fallen wizard's presentation of reality in its proper form:

> "The words of this wizard stand on their heads," he growled, gripping the handle of his axe. "In the language of Orthanc help means ruin, and saving means slaying, that is plain" (II, 235).

And when Theodan, too, rejects the spell, after listening to Saruman's wily voice, the watching men see Saruman break into anger, and "to some suddenly it seemed that they saw a snake coiling to strike." Men accept for themselves the spells that bind them, and the wizard had been using the power of self-imposed images to delude his listeners. And he, of course, is caught in his own delusion, that what he has created as an image is reality. The wizard is trapped in a world he has made and which he hates: "Before he could conceal it, they saw through the mask the anguish of a mind in doubt, loathing to stay and dreading to leave its refuge" (II, 239). Those who misuse their power are not only divided themselves, but unhappy prisoners of their own works. They are not free to know the joy of sharing in the life of the whole world, since their interest only in the self has taken them outside the pale of the world community. Shut up in his lonely tower with his creature, Wormtongue, Saruman is the "other side" of Gandalf, an example of a wizard who has gone against his true nature. Pride in his ability to use words, to make images, has resulted in bondage to himself. The lonely tower, the *palentir* in which the Eye roves alone over the world, the dead matter out of which Saruman has built machines and prisons—these are the conventional images drawn from traditions of magic and stories of the imagination which Tolkien uses to express the psychology of a perverted life.

The contrast between Gandalf's control over his power and Saruman's loss of control is worked out throughout the Trilogy. We see a similar contrast in Gandalf's confrontation with the Balrog of Morgoth in Orc-occupied Moria, where "the world is gnawed by nameless things."

The Balrog is an unnatural creature, brought to the upper world by Sauron's increased activity, and it has something of the shapelessness of Sin and Death in *Paradise Lost*, who are also unnatural creations following upon the perversion of the good by Satan. Tolkien also uses this technique of representing the supreme evil, the dissolution of form into formlessness, in his figure of the Black Prince, the leader of the Ringwraiths or Nazgûls, who leads the attack on Minas Tirith; the Black Prince wears a crown but no face is to be seen beneath it. The vague picture we receive of Sauron is yet another example of this technique, as we shall see.

The battle between the monstrous Balrog and Gandalf is significant because as a consequence, Gandalf is dragged into the depths of the earth. A struggle follows between the power of formlessness or chaos, and that of form in the primal depths of creation, "beyond light and knowledge." And there, Gandalf tells the reassembled Fellowship long after they had thought him lost forever, he defeated the Balrog in a purely physical, knockdown-dragout battle. Tolkien makes the description brief but in the epic tradition in which it is cast, the mountains were "crowned with storm. Thunder they heard and lightning, they said, smote upon Celebdil, and leaped back broken into tongues of fire" (I, 429). Gandalf proves the stronger and throws his enemy down the mountain; white magic proves stronger than black in the master-plan of the Third Age. But it is important that the two opposing forces, thus personified, fight a real, physical battle, exactly as the allies against the Dark Lord must be prepared to fight real battles in which men may die. Gandalf's fight with the Balrog is patterned after a long tradition of such spiritual warfare; the spirit finds its expression in form, in matter, in the shapes of men and things. In *Beowulf*, the dragon at last drives its tusks into the hero's neck; "he staggered; the blood/Came flooding forth, fell like rain" (ll.2692–3). In the biblical story of Jacob, the father of the Israelites wrestles with an angel all night, and neither can win by throwing the other. Spiritual purposes must often be fulfilled by "wrestling" with evil, in the perverted forms it assumes. The mightiest in knowledge must not be less weak in actual strength; the ability of Gandalf to "wrestle" with the Balrog denies the helplessness of men before the threat of chaos. This is a triumph of the will, power asserted to perfect and cleanse the world.

And Gandalf himself passes through a "cleansing" process whose form is borrowed from sacrificial rites the world over: after the struggle to disperse chaos or give form, the "hero" is himself changed for a higher nature, but one implicit in his natural self. Gandalf, after the battle,

> "strayed out of thought and time, and I wandered far on roads that I will not tell, . . . Naked I was sent back—for a brief time, until my task was done. And naked I lay upon the mountain-top. The tower behind was crumbled into dust, the window gone; the ruined stair was choked with burned and broken stone. I was alone, forgotten, without escape upon the hard horn of the world. There I lay staring upward, while the stars wheeled over, and each day was as long as a life-age of the earth. Faint to my ears came the gathered rumor of all lands: the springing and the dying, the song and the weeping, and the slow everlasting groan of overburdened stone" (II, 135).

Though he is from beyond Middle-earth and, we must assume, immortal, the wizard must still pass through a purgation in which he plays the role of a type of Christ. He symbolically "gives up" the world; time stands still; earth loses all her beauty and her life-giving qualities for the suffering soul. This pattern of death and rebirth is familiar to readers of Quest literature, and while Tolkien does not make much of Gandalf's experience as he does of the mortal and suffering Frodo, this moment of mystical loss and reintegration is a metamorphosis analogous to others in *The Lord of the Ring*. A critic has pointed out that this is a "death" for the world community, a loss of the world for the good of life; Gandalf's seeming death and resurrection is a paradigm, of the passage of the mythic hero through the underworld to return with the triumph of new knowledge for his people. [16] Gandalf the Grey becomes Gandalf the White, the fusing of all colors in the One. He is thus prepared by the powers of the world to combat the Dark Lord as a pure and alternate spirit. And his wisdom takes the form of willed action: he stands against the hosts of Mordor during the seige of Minas Tirith, and his will holds the invading forces of the enemy at bay long enough for Rohan and the forces of Aragorn to arrive with aid; he holds Gondor together until Aragorn can assume his rightful place as King, and confronts the defeatist position of the last steward, Denethor. It is Gandalf who can now see into the Dark Lord's mind, outguessing him, directing the strategy of the Allies against Mordor until Frodo and Sam can achieve the end of the Ring.

Gandalf is the artist working with words, with the imagination, to affect the lives of created beings. His metamorphosis is available to everyone with a true self to be realized. Hence Gandalf's participation in that "Joy" Tolkien describes in "On Fairy-Stories." We see this in his speech, in the tone of his voice, often sardonic and humorous, poking fun at the pompous or the overbearing, never mean, a little weary. Gandalf laughs at Saruman pontificating on his tower, and the fallen wizard's fantasies "vanished like a puff of smoke." Following the first interview of Gandalf and Pippin with Denethor, Pippin sees under the lines of care and sorrow in the wizard's face "that under all there was a great joy: a fountain of mirth enough to set a kingdom laughing, were it to gush forth" (III, 34). This is the power of the imagination to sustain its believers.

Chapter Five: Men and Others

The figures or "races" drawn from traditional mythic sources and Tolkien's imagination—hobbits, dwarves, elves, wizards—are all, in a sense, transitional; their work on Middle-earth will end with the Third Age and mortal Men will rule in the age to follow. But this does not mean that the tasks will be different. The men who appear in *The Lord of the Rings* are also part of the movement of history and must be Guardians of the imaginative vision and of the earth in which it finds expression. Readers of the Trilogy must be impressed with Aragorn as with Frodo and Sam, and Gandalf; for the man who is to be King Elessar is represented as a man of action, who can *do* meaningful deeds against evil in the world; his presentation as a warrior is only as important as his respect for other created beings, his care for the hobbits; his respect for the complexity, the beauty, the sources of being and power that made him and which he protects and encourages. Aragorn, the most important man in *The Lord of the Rings*, represents the Guardian's responsibility for the world. He is also archetypally human in his developing identity; like other fairy-story heroes his true birth and identity as heir to the throne are hidden from other men, and blossom slowly through the trials of suffering, of leadership, of battle that prove his worth. He is thus part of the theme of inner reality realized through outward struggle. Again (and this is significant for the twentieth century), Aragorn comes to the full reality of his nature as a *political* figure in whom civilization asserts its ordering power over chaos. The new king of Gondor is both the heir to long centuries of civilized rule and the initiator of a new age; he is both an end and a means to that end, in a very different sense than Saruman's. The ability to speak to other kinds of living beings, to imagine the free lives of others different from oneself is essential to life in Middle-earth. Aragorn as King Elessar is both the true prince revealed after a life of disguise and the affirmation of man's ability to rule himself and others through adherence to just laws. In this respect, other men in the Trilogy are used for contrast: Theoden, the Lord of the Mark of Rohan who rules a tribal community in which horses and honor are the principles of social organization; and Denethor, the Steward of Gondor, and his two sons, Boromir and Faramir. These men have the responsibility of preserving their respective lands, and so continue the theme of the wise exercise of power we have been following. But where Aragorn has developed control over himself and a strong will in the face of adversity, Denethor and Boromir both succumb to the temptations of power, and become agents for Sauron. Finally, it is Aragorn's return to the throne of his fathers, thus fulfilling the historical development of the Third Age, which initiates the apocalypse and the recovery of civilization in the city of God on earth, Minas Tirith.

Like other "lost" princes, Aragorn lives a hidden life in the wilds of Middle-earth, as a Ranger. But the Rangers, like Gandalf, are also Guardians protecting the Shire, among other places, from the growing Shadow of Sauron. He is called "Strider" and is the descendant of the ancient Numenoreans and the High Elves, once rulers of Arnor, the Northern Kingdom, which has vanished from history. The Rangers are left on the edges of civilization to guard it, and for Aragorn to await the moment of his destiny. The metamorphosis which Aragorn undergoes from "Strider" to King Elessar is the development of the truth hidden within him. His disguises as Strider or a member of the Fellowship of the Ring are both protection and a means of discovering his true self. For like Ralph in Morris' *The Well at the World's End*, Aragorn goes under other names than his princely one in order to prove himself as a man. But in Tolkien's scheme of values the heroic warfare against the monster or the enemy is less a test of Man than is the gentler concern shown for his fellow created beings. Strider shows his imaginative power in his care for the hobbits on their journey to Rivendell and later when he determines to rescue Merry and Pippin from the orcs. He is a fighter, wielding the Sword-That-Was-Broken, but he fights as a healer and comforter, finding the special herb to place on Frodo's wound (never to fully heal) after the battle before Weathertop; and again, when Minas Tirith has been saved, laying his royal and healing hands on the wounded. Here, in the legendary application of the kingsfoil, Tolkien is chiefly concerned to illustrate the healing power of love for others.

Like other heroes with imaginative power, Aragorn is a part of the legend-making world. He marries the dream princess, Arwen Undomiel; he tells the hobbits the elvishly sentimental tale of the meeting of the mortal man Beren and the immortal princess Luthien Tinuviel, who gives up her immortality for him, a conscious choice for love. Aragorn is descended from this legendary pair, and so their history lives in him: his telling of their tale, and his own life are the same thing. History is not dead, but lives in its descendants who can make use of it, becoming the guardians of *its* power. Aragorn, marrying Arwen, repeats the history of his ancestors. Frodo finds Aragorn with a flower of the elf-world, *elanor*, in his hand, dreaming of Arwen:

> He was wrapped in some fair memory: and as
> Frodo looked at him he knew that he beheld
> things as they once had been in this same place.
> For the grim years were removed from the face
> of Aragorn, and he seemed clothed in white,
> a young lord tall and fair . . . (I, 456).

Memory, like the lore of the past for Gandalf, can give meaning to the present, even to the recreation of the lore-master himself. Aragorn's "vision" on the hill of Amroth is also his true nature, that of a "young lord tall and fair," a metaphor for his appearance when he finally ascends the throne of Gondor and seems to all the beholders "yet in the flower of manhood" (III, 304). Cosmic order is affirmed through such a revelation, and the lost prince assumes his true "shape" in returning to his ancestral one.

Another element in Aragorn's presentation which must be noted is the exercise of the *will* which identifies him; and the converse of this, his ability to control, to order, the power he has been given. [17] As *The Lord of the Rings* progresses, Aragorn becomes increasingly distant from the reader, less a thoughtful, searching human being and more the ideal king. This is intentional on Tolkien's part; he wishes to provide Middle-earth with a political figure expressive of the order in society and Nature which has triumphed over chaos. We find this figure often in fantasy, in myth and literature. King Arthur of Tennyson's *Idylls of the King* is perhaps most familiar: a paternal figure who is above the passions and desperate heroism of his youth and whose wisdom and inspiration hold the society together. As the True Prince, Aragorn must sum up the virtues and the faith of his people, for whom he is not only the leader but also the expression of their imaginative power. And under such responsibility, Tolkien carefully "leads" him into the idealized being he must be, "tall as the sea-kings of old" and "ancient of days." At the same time, it is Aragorn's *will*, his fated and purposive choice of alternatives, which fulfills his being and that of the society he is destined to govern.

The concept of the "will" in the Trilogy and in *The Hobbit*, too, is the assertion of the true self, a faithful statement of oneself in a world threatened by an external power who appears all too persuasive. Will means helping others, perhaps commanding them to achieve their true nature and being in the world; but also means control of the fear, the passion, the possibilities for evil which break down the self and open it to invasion by another will. Basically, Tolkien is arguing for a kind of Renaissance vision of man as a proud, self-confident individual *within* a unified society whose structure gives a place and a sense of individual worth to all its members. Aragorn as the king must help create, or re-create, this society through his own will, living up to the expectations inherent in his nature.

Hence another value in the medieval setting which dominates the last books of *The Lord of the Rings*. For the medieval tradition provides us with wise or evil rulers, and with companies of men, like the Fellowship of the Ring, who are ruled by the will of their lord, and owe allegiance to him, allegiance which defines their place in the society. Thus the great battles at Helm's Deep or before the gates of Minas Tirith are valuable in constructing the Secondary World of the novel because we see there the physical expression of a spiritual and imaginative struggle. But we also bring to these battles our reading in Sir Walter Scott or *The Fairy Queen*, which express the will of the good ruler or knight in sword and tournament. Such battles are basically less interesting than the individual struggles of Frodo or even Bilbo. But the battles are as much part of the total picture of Middle-earth as the inner struggle of the post-medieval hero like Frodo.

Tolkien pursues this point. Frodo's control over the Ring must be an act of will, his own. After he has put on

141

the Ring to escape the pursuing Black Riders, only to reveal himself to them and be wounded, Frodo "regretted his foolishness, and reproached himself for weakness of will; for he now perceived that in putting on the Ring he obeyed not his own desire but the commanding wish of his enemies" (I, 266). And in similar passages throughout the Quest, his will struggles, not always successfully, to assert itself against the pull of the Ring and the watchful Eye of Sauron. Frodo is, after all, a Halfling, with certain all-too-human tendencies; Aragorn is destined to be king, and his will grows increasingly strong: the ancient swords and crystal balls borrowed from medieval and magical trappings by Tolkien are but the counters with which his will proves itself. Before the final contest with Sauron, Aragorn shows himself in the *palentir*, something not even Gandalf could do, hoping not only to upset the plans of the Dark Lord who must fear the coming of Isildur's heir, but also to assert his will against the Enemy in the magical stone:

> "I am the lawful master of the Stone, and I had both the right and the strength to use it, or so I judged. The right cannot be doubted. The strength was enough—barely. . . . It was a bitter struggle, and the weariness is slow to pass. I spoke no word to him, and in the end I wrenched the Stone to my own will. . . . Now in the very hour of his great designs the heir of Isildur and the Sword are revealed; for I showed the blade re-forged to him. He is not so mighty yet that he is above fear; nay, doubt ever gnaws him" (III, 62–3).

The True Prince controls the things that rightfully belong to him, and he returns the *palentir* to its purpose as an instrument for guarding the land, as no one else could do. With the effort of will on Aragorn's part comes a corresponding increase in the knowledge, and so in his power: "When I had mastered the Stone, I learned many things." Each act of strength and goodness on the part of the True Prince increases his power. On the other hand, evil deeds, too, snowball, and reduce the chances of escape from an evil nature. The Dark Riders who become Ring-wraiths were once mortal men whose pursuit of power through the Ring made them vulnerable to Sauron and finally destroyed them as human beings.

What Aragorn learns, in his contest with Sauron, is that the Enemy can be outguessed, and put on the defensive by the Allies. And it is then that Aragorn determines to pursue the prophetic advice to enter the Paths of the Dead and call the Oath-breakers to his aid. These are the ghosts of a vanished army which defected when Isildur needed them in battle ages before, and are under his curse. After death they must live as spirits on earth until they are called once more to fight against Sauron; they will have then fulfilled their oath and cancelled their status in Limbo. Aragorn proceeds to seek this phantom army in the Halls of the Dead, leading them out on the other side of the mountains to do battle with Sauron's allies. They are then dismissed, having fulfilled their oath, and Aragorn goes on to take command of the army going in relief of the siege of Minas Tirith. Tolkien does not make as much of Aragorn's journey through the world of the near-Dead as he might have; the theme of the oath-breakers goes back a long way in tradition to the myths of troops pledged to a hero like Beowulf, who fail him in danger. The passage of the living through the underground has its precedents in the apocryphal Harrowing of Hell by Christ and in the visits of Ulysses and Aeneas to the Underworld. Like the underground struggle of Gandalf against the Balrog, such a journey can be symbolic of death and rebirth. In this episode, however, it is important for its statement about Aragorn: "and such was the strength of his will in that hour that all the Dunedain and their horses followed him. . . . only his will held them to go on. No other mortal Men could have endured it . . ." (III,70,75). And when Legolas the elf describes the troops of the Dead marching to battle under the future King Elessar's command, he says: "In that hour I looked on Aragorn and thought how great and terrible a Lord he might have become in the strength of his will, had he taken the Ring to himself. Not for naught does Mordor fear him. But nobler in his spirit than the understanding of Sauron . . ." (III, 186). Like Galadriel and Gandalf, Aragorn the Man has been wise enough to control the desire for power, to be bigger than he is, to resist desiring the Ring, which no being, however great, may wield without destroying or perverting his true nature. Through his own efforts as the disguised but true ruler Aragorn takes over the military power of Gondor and its allies, and so through action in the real world, he asserts his right to rule. Aragorn's Quest differs from that of the dwarves in *The Hobbit*, who selfishly seek to recover the material possessions of the past; and from that of Frodo, who seeks to destroy the past. Aragorn fulfills history and returns Middle-earth to the cherished creation of the imagination.

Theoden, King of the Mark of Rohan, at first appears to have fallen from his task as a Guardian through the evil advice of Wormtongue, a creature of Saruman's. But under Gandalf's counsel he joins the Allies to die with honor on the battlefield. It is Denethor, the Steward of Gondor, who fails in his task, for in using his great wisdom and the *palentir* to spy on Sauron and perhaps counter the Dark Lord's power, he becomes increasingly pessimistic of success. At last when he is needed on the field of battle, he commits suicide on the funeral pyre planned for his wounded son, Faramir. His is the sin of despair: "Why should we wish to live longer? Why should we not go to death side by side?" (III,157) Gandalf's answer denies even this:

> "And only the heathen kings, under the domination of the Dark Power, did thus, slaying themselves in pride and despair, murdering their kin to ease their own death" (III,157).

Pride in one's wisdom or power can become self-destructive through the despair that follows failure.

Tolkien has always been interested in this moral twist; in his essay on "Ofermod" (*Tolkien Reader*, pp. 19–24), he discusses the "excess" of chivalric pride in such Anglo-

Saxon heroes as Beowulf, a self-confident challenging of fate which is more than the courage demanded, and is harmful to the society dependent upon his strength. This is the power of the will uncontrolled. Boromir, Denethor's son, dies in an attempt to take the One Ring from Frodo, even though he had sworn an oath to preserve the Fellowship and defend the Ringbearer. He, too, desires excessive power: "How I would drive the hosts of Mordor, and all men would flock to my banner!" (I, 515) And he sees himself "a mighty king, benevolent and wise." In writing about early Anglo-Saxon views of the hero, Tolkien notes that the hero is often to be praised, but also condemned, for he has sought personal glory. Beorhtnoth, in "The Battle of Malden" wanted to make a " 'sporting fight' on level terms" with the invading Danes, "but at other people's expense. . . . he was responsible for all the men under him, not to throw away their lives except with one object, the defence of the realm from an implacable foe." Thus honor becomes a motive in itself, endangering the future of the kingdom of which he is the guardian: "Magnificent perhaps, but certainly wrong" (*Tolkien Reader*, pp. 21–2). This inherited attitude toward pride is exactly what the author of *The Lord of the Rings* has been working with all along, and in bringing the theme of excessive pride into his Trilogy, Tolkien has placed it in the "main stream" of English literature. Any passion which goes uncontrolled, which leads its possessor to leave his place in the social, political and cosmic schema, is destructive of that schema. "It is a joy," say Theoden's people upon his recovery to take the helm of his country again, "to see you return into your own." Excessive pride denies the network of responsibilities, of friendships, of the sharing of civilization. A careful balance between autonomy and responsibility is essential, controlled by the discerning and ordering will of Man. This is also the freedom the imagination promises.

We have seen that when created beings begin to surrender their essential selves to the Dark Power outside them, "things" begin to take over, perverted into instruments of evil. Thus the One Ring becomes a directing and coercive force; the trees in the Old Forest take on destructive life beyond their natures. However, Tolkien has been careful to round out the picture of the natural Guardians in Middle-earth with images drawn from Nature: the Shire with its rural beauty and productivity; Lórien with the heightened colors and odors of trees and flowers. There the grass is as "green as Spring-time in the Elder days" and the colors of flowers seem "fresh and poignant" as though first perceived by man in the Garden of Eden: "In winter here no heart could mourn for summer or for spring. No blemish or sickness or deformity could be seen in anything that grew upon the earth" (I, 454–5). Such natural loveliness is in part the care of the hobbits or elves. But Tolkien has also created Guardians from out of Nature itself, in the ents, a dwindling tribe of "tree-shepherds" who live in Fangorn Forest, and who turn up at a time when the Quest seems frustrated by orcs and Ringwraiths, and before Saruman has been overcome. The ents are nearly trees themselves, and so occupy that borderline in the imagination between what we can imagine and what Nature actually presents. As Tolkien has noted, we wish to be able to speak to other living things, and the ents realize our wish that trees, customarily inarticulate and immobile, speak and move. Trees have long symbolized life itself. The Tree of Life grew in the Garden of Eden next to the fatal Tree of Knowledge, and in the forest cultures of Western Europe trees provided on the one hand lumber for houses and boats, civilized things, and, on the other, the last retreats for all that was mysterious, frightening, hidden in the shadows. We wish trees could speak, but this is the converse of what we know: that they keep secrets. The forest is older than men, but where it gave way before their advance, like all guilty conquerors, men endowed the old trees with their own visions.

Maltreated, Nature can become perverted and turn against life. Old Man Willow, whom the hobbits meet deep in the Old Forest, is the malicious relic of the magnificent past. The barren wastes that surround the Emyn Muil or the slagheaps and deserts of Mordor reflect the barren minds that have ceased to exercise that ordered benevolence which Guardians like Gandalf and Aragorn assert. However, the ents return to the half-lit land of humanlike action and speech, and realize our wish for help from the vegetable world. Tree-shepherds, they tend their flocks of trees not because it is sound economic policy but because trees are beautiful and respond to love and attention; nothing in Middle-earth is originally alien to a grand design.

The ents, oldest living things, appear simple and rather archaic on the surface. Slow of movement, it takes them a long time to decide a question and to speak to the point in their ancient and long worded language. The Ent-moot, or council, which Treebeard organizes, is a kind of parody of the various Councils held by the Allies throughout *The Lord of the Rings*. But their life in the depths of Fangorn suggests a race closer to primitive, "natural" life than man, a life lived by strange, slow-moving giants in the forest of the mind. Their leader, Fangorn or Treebeard, is "at least" fourteen feet high. It is hard to tell if he is wearing green and grey bark, or if this is his skin. His beard is "bushy, almost twiggy at the roots, thin and mossy at the ends." Here, of course, Tolkien is letting the metaphor of vegetation describe this giant for him. And as with all creatures who have survived through the ages of Middle-earth, Treebeard has the remarkable eyes of the immortal or nearly immortal:

> One felt as if there was an enormous well behind them, filled up with ages of memory and long, slow, steady thinking; but their surface was sparkling with the present: like sun shimmering on the outer leaves of a vast tree, or on the ripples of a very deep lake. . . . it felt as if something that grew in the ground—asleep, you might say, or just feeling itself as something between root-tip and leaf-tip, between deep earth and sky—had suddenly waked up, and was considering you with the same slow care that it had given to its own inside affairs for endless years (II, 83).

147

As with the elves, time has brought a diminution of power; the ents are dwindling in number, in part because they are turning into trees, "growing sleepy going tree-ish, as you might say. . . . Some are quite wide awake, and a few are, well, ah, well, getting *Entish*. That is going on all the time. When that happens to a tree you find that some have bad hearts." Many of their trees, in turn, can talk to their shepherds, a mutual coordination available between beings and environment when the imagination is still a way of life. The ents who survive have a knowledge of themselves, an inner strength, which is in part a product of thinking about the past self built up like the inner rings of a tree, year after year. Unlike others who must read lore or search the past, they *are* the past, living metaphors.

Tolkien handles this beautifully with his description of Entish, their elf-derived language that is, like the ents themselves, the culmination of long ages of thought and experience. They have not shortened their words or speech with their decline. Rather the ent tongue carries with it all the past experience of the world, and the words are compounds of many-nuanced expressions to capture every shade of meaning. "Treebeard" is a shortening of Fangorn's real name, which probably takes hours to say. This keeps it secret and yet personal, and we know the importance of the secret name in this society. "Taurelilomea-tumbalemorna Tumbaletaurea Lomeanor," in Entish, means "Forestmanyshadoweddeepvalleyblack Deepvalley-forested Gloomy-land," by which Treebeard is saying that "there is a black shadow in the deep dales of the forest" (III, 510). Such language is not just spoken; it "takes place," it occurs. The poetry of the ents is long-lined, free in its rhythms and filled with sonorous place-names, evidence of a race that has remained in one place for ages. And the ents are naturally strong on ceremony, the enactment of civilization's needs in a ritual form; decorum is the rule.

In the Ent-moot, the formal language of the ents comes out as a chant: "first one joined and then another, until they were all chanting together in a long rising and falling rhythm, now louder on one side of the ring, now dying away there and rising to a great boom on the other side." Where all is ceremony, the life force can sometimes be dried up in conventions of life and language. But Tolkien's view of History, as we have seen, is that it can not only be "imagined," and turned to legend and tradition; it also affects the present. The ents, aroused by Saruman's destruction of the forests they guard, take action and move out into the light of the present. Like the elves or the Men who guarded Mordor, they had become careless of their trust. When they are aroused at last and descend on Isengard and release the waters to drown Saruman's machines and wolf dens, the ents prove their power, applied with frightening determination. Symbolically, theirs is the triumph of living, organic, heart-felt Nature over the rational, mechanical, inorganic world of machines and science which had been put to "unnatural" purposes by the power-hungary wizard. Power for the ents is a low-keyed but beautifully coordinated image of what the world is, expressed in care for their "flock" and in their language, in their very being, the combination of wisdom and joy we observed in Gandalf. Their lack of interest in the created, the crafted, in gold or in political power, interestingly enough keeps them from being part of the Dark Lord's scheme, but it also removes them from the arena of government which Men must exercise in the larger sphere beyond the forest. The ents' pastoral community complements the re-established kingdom of Gondor; it does not supplant it.

Poetry is available to the ents not only in their own lives, and language, but in their sexual history. There are no more "entlings" or young ents because the entwives, long ago, went away and have never been found again. The ents are all bachelors living alone in their caves among the trees in a manner which suggests Tolkien's approval of their lives. But the loss of the entwives gives the picture of the ents a touch of that romantic sentimentality with which the past is so often colored in *The Lord of the Rings*: "There were entmaidens then: ah! the loveliness of Fimbrethil, of Wandlimb the lightfooted, in the days of our youth!" But as Treebeard explains, the entwives did not want to live in the forests, but out on the plains where they might cultivate gardens, and make things grow: "They did not desire to speak with these things; but they wished them to hear and obey what was said to them. . . . for the entwives desired order, and plenty, and peace (by which they meant that things should remain where they had set them). So the entwives made gardens to live in." Finally, the gardenmakers, who have taught their craft to men, disappear; their gardens are destroyed in a war and become the Brown Lands; the entwives have never returned to the forests where the ents continue to live in secret. "We believe that we may meet again in a time to come, and perhaps we shall find somewhere a land where we can live together and both be content. But it is forboded that that will only be when we have both lost all that we now have" (II, 99–100).

Hidden in this charming history is Tolkien's version of a myth about the founding of civilization when gardening replaced gathering food in the wild. But the author's sympathies obviously lie with the ents; if nothing else, they have produced some lovely poetry from their loss. More importantly, perhaps, is the ents' "tale" as part of the complex web of mythic relationships Tolkien weaves, tying together the fate of the various races in parallel accounts. But among other things, *The Lord of the Rings* is about love and friendship possible not only among various kinds of beings, as with Legolas the Elf and Gimli the Dwarf. It is also about commitment to love and friendship as one of the deepest elements of life itself. One thing that makes the Trilogy so popular is its frankly sentimental but heartfelt statements which living beings make about each other. In an age when few people are able to express their emotions, their affection for one another, or even to feel emotions, the openness of shared feeling is especially attractive. Aragorn's concern for the little hobbits is part of his ability to rule. The Fellowship of the Ring is more than an epic convention; it is expressive of the deep love for others which is the soundest basis for government. The oath the members of the Fellowship take to go with the Ring-bearer to the South is expressive of a heartfelt loyalty. For the most part, those who attempt to do evil are loners, wandering outside the circle of civilization like the monster Grendel in *Beowulf,* like his malevolent counterpart in Tolkien, the Gollum.

Save one. Tom Bombadil lives with Goldberry in the heart of the Old Forest and is presented as a kind of spirit of nature who is untouched by Sauron's will to power. He is so completely a part of Nature that power is not an issue for him. As Goldberry explains, he is the "Master" of the world of the Old Forest, but he does not own it: "The trees and the grasses and all things growing or living in the land belong each to themselves" (I, 174). He is a kind of daimonic being who lived before history, "before the river and the trees" existed on the earth. Tom Bombadil can live with the trees of the Old Forest, even rotten, malevolent Old Willow, because he is wholly a spirit of joy, beyond good and evil, taking Nature as it is. Like the other "good" figures of Middle-earth, however, he too, is a Guardian, harvesting the flowers and fruits of the wilderness, rescuing hobbits from trees and the wraiths of the Barrow-downs. He is totally unaffected by the attractive power of the One Ring: indeed, he can make *it* disappear, and even see Frodo wearing it when the others cannot. The test of his fusion of self and imagination lies in his songs and in his speech which, when scanned, is almost entirely poetry, and may be measured in metrical feet. But, on the other hand, Tom is not concerned with the struggle against Sauron. He bears responsibility for his world, but nothing more, because he is beyond the necessity of choice and of active construction of a civilized response to Sauron. He has that holy Joy which lies at the basis of life, but in a political moment at the end of an age, this is not enough.

Joy, on the other hand, is not available to the evil beings allied with Sauron in Middle-earth. Theirs is a deadness at the heart symbolized by the Old Willow which snatches at the inexperienced hobbits; his destructive spirit has spread through the forest until all its trees are under his "dominion." The deadening of the heart is both a cause and a consequence of the will to dominate other beings, to limit their individual freedom for one's own ends. The Old Willow has nothing but anger, spite, hatred for living things that can walk freely and happily on the earth. Once, however, it was a green, lovely tree in the great forests that spread over the earth. Now it takes someone full of joy like Tom Bombadil to control Old Willow. Again, the dead heart appears in the Ringwraiths or Nazgûl who change from "Mortal Men" to unnatural creatures, winged, featureless zombies without wills of their own. Their captain appears as the Lord of the Nazgûl before the gates of Minas Tirith wearing a kingly crown, "and yet upon no head visible was it set. The red fires shone between it and the mantled shoulders vast and dark. From a mouth unseen there came a deadly laughter" (III, 125). The rotten heart of the willow and the headless rider both represent the same thing; evil is the perversion of the will through the pursuit of power, and a consequent turning away from God through pride in the self. A long Christian tradition defines evil as a negative, the absence of goodness in created beings who lose their true natures as they were made, and become twisted, often formless parodies of their essential beings. The Nazgûl were not originally evil beings but mortal men tempted by the rings into trying to be more than themselves.

In the beginning, then, evil did not exist; nothing was *made* evil. As Elrond tells the assembled council, as long as the Ring "is in the world it will be a danger even to the Wise. For nothing is evil in the beginning. Even Sauron himself is described as a "servant or emissary" (III, 190), a "tool" of some larger power. The perverted will begins to provide shapes for evil. We see this in Saruman whose will for power leads him to create a desert at Isengard and a special race of orcs to inhabit it. We see this potential in Bilbo and Frodo. As the Ring gives them power, so they must pay for it, and Bilbo's invisibility, his life "out of time" shared by his fellow hobbits, is paid for by becoming "thin and stretched," not like his true self. Evil is not, in Tolkien's reading, original with the creation of the world. But it must inevitably arise in a world where created beings are free to make choices, to exercise their free wills in a series of decisions which will either enlarge their imaginative life or narrow and pervert it. This is the ancient paradox of freedom, in that men (or in Tolkien's version, all created beings) must be free to choose the good on their own; they cannot be directed against their will. And so, of course, they may choose to do evil, usually through pride and a consequent failure to respect and cherish the rich, imaginative freedom of other created beings. Those who choose to do evil, as we have said, keep cutting down their freedom until they can be said to have no will left for choosing. Sooner or later, says Gandalf, he who uses the One Ring, as Bilbo and Frodo now and then do, "becomes . . . invisible, and walks in the twilight under the eye of the dark power that Rules the Rings." To become invisible is to be without form, a tangible part of the community of imaginative beings, secret, hidden, alone, in isolated pride. The One Ring does Sauron's work since it binds those it attracts to their own self-conceit. If the Ring can be destroyed, then the Dark Lord's power will crumble, "and he will be maimed forever, becoming a mere spirit of malice that gnaws itself in the shadows, but cannot again grow or take shape," for Sauron had put his strength into it (III, 190). And it is the "taking shape" which is important, for when a dream or an idea takes form, as the One Ring is a "form" for Sauron its maker, then the will and the imagination can deal with it.

Appropriately, then, Sauron is never revealed in a final "form": he always appears as a concept, a "darkness," a *name* which lives in the minds of others. He is a *thought* in the minds of those who have given themselves to him. In so doing, they have begun the process of narrowing the imagination until they have become "things" animated only by the thought of their master. Thus Sauron never appears in *The Lord of the Rings*; his messengers are the Black Riders or the hordes of orcs and enslaved peoples who come to represent his power in concrete military or social form. Like Smaug in *The Hobbit*, he exists because he is called into being by the desires of others. But also like Smaug, he is a power once he gains control of the lives of others. Tolkien symbolizes Sauron's power in the Eye which appears on uniforms and shields, and more importantly, in the *palentir* when Pippin looks into it; or in Frodo's mind, when on the top of Amon Hen he has a vision of the world advancing to war and suddenly "feels" the Eye of Sauron searching for him. "A fierce eager will was there." It comes leaping toward him, for Frodo has made himself available for identification as the Ring-bearer by putting on the Ring for invisibility to others (I, 519). Guilt feels the Eye seeking it out, exposing secrets, expressing all that is inevitable in the destructive *will* of another: a "deadly gaze, naked, immovable" (II, 301). This Lidless Eye, is, of course, the perfect symbol of the police state, of those societies ruled by fear so that no one dare be individual or utter criticism of the mysterious leaders hidden behind castle walls. It is also expressive of the paradox of evil, because the servants of the Ring enter a world invisible to those as yet free. When Bilbo and Frodo wear the Ring separating themselves from the natural life of their fellow beings, they remain visible to the Black Riders and the Eye of Sauron. It is to Tolkien's credit as a fantasist that he can give us the *effect* of evil in pursuit of Frodo without describing Sauron; what men believe evil can do is important, and any more exact physical description of the Devil would be less convincing than the varied forms which evil takes in its adherents.

But "varied forms" may be the wrong words, for the creatures of Sauron are notoriously conformist and uniform in their self-destruction. Sauron's flaw is his desire for power, a desire of which he is a prisoner. The Dark Lord sees everything in terms of what he himself wants, in terms of the spies, the depraved beings, the vast armies he has assembled. He cannot imagine other beings acting for other ends, to be themselves, in fact; he believes that since he wants power, so do they. Since he wants the One Ring, so must they. Consequently, he cannot imagine that Allies mean to destroy the Ring. Nor can he foresee, for all his spies and his searching Eye, how love and hobbit fortitude and even "chance" can overthrow the best laid plans. Gandalf sees this, a being capable of the best imaginative "tricks," as a wizard, a "magic-and-games" maker:

"Well, let folly be our cloak, a veil before the eyes of the Enemy! For he is very wise, and weighs all things to a nicety in the scales of his malice. But the only measure that he knows is desire, desire for power; and so he judges all hearts" (I, 353).

And this "foolish" reasoning works. The Dark Lord cannot, for instance, imagine hobbits; when he has finally discovered their existence, Frodo escapes by chance or his own willed effort from the trap. Because Sauron cannot imagine or respect the life of others, they get away from him, however great the temptation each feels to give up, to surrender to the greater Will they must otherwise continuously combat.

We can also look at evil not only as a threat and a challenge to the imaginative being. We can consider the necessity of giving evil form so that it can be dealt with. Thus the past, that "Shadow," haunts the lives of created beings as History; when it appears as the One Ring, or the Black Riders in pursuit of the Ring-bearer, we can begin to come to grips with its influence. Error is given form in order to be corrected or destroyed. We have seen how the perverted men, the Black Riders, change their appearance until their leader appears, headless, before the gates of Minas Tirith. Then Gandalf the White can confront him for the first time. Then he can be destroyed. Eowyn, the virgin warrior, symbolic of purity and inspired by her love for Aragorn, destroys him as no man could have. She is helped by Merry the Hobbit; between them, they literally "cut him down" at the time when he is at his greatest power, "ripe" in his pride. And when he least expects attack by a disguised woman and a halfling. But the "accident" works, and with his death, his mantel and hauberk fall shapeless upon the ground: "and a cry went up into the shuddering air, and faded to a shrill wailing, passing with the wind, a voice bodiless and thin that died, and was swallowed up and was never heard again in that age of this world" (III, 143).

Sauron works with two kinds of creatures, those whose

bent to his Will is strong in them and those which he creates and who have no choices to make. Like all such creatures, they are made "in his image," and so give form to his own perverse nature. The orcs are made, Tree-beard tells us, in imitation of elves. Where the latter are of the air and light, spiritual, ultimately transcendent and immortal, the orcs are gross in body, fear the light, and seem conceived, like Caliban in *The Tempest*, as of the earth, the earth seen as a base or vile substance rather than created by God. Orcs are perversions of true being. Living in the mines of Moria, in tunnels, they never appear singly, but in troops at the command of brutal leaders, and have no individual qualities. Beaten and beating, they seem a kind of compound of cavemen and totalitarian army. Where the elves eat *lembas* which gives life, the orcs, like those raised to live in the light by Saruman, the Uruk-hai, eat the flesh of men; and others eat their own kind. This cannibalism is symbolic of the nature of perverted beings who have no respect even for themselves.

Orcs are a terrifying creation because of their brutality, and because of the powerful sense of their presence when they mass in pursuit. Hoard after hoard of orcs charge to their destruction, pouring by the hour from the Black Gate of Mordor; because of their lack of any individualizing qualities, they seem undefeatable, a great creeping scum over the earth.

> Against the Deeping Wall the hosts of Isengard roared like a sea. Orcs and hillmen swarmed about its feet from end to end. Ropes with grappling hooks were hurled over the parapet faster than men could cut them or fling them back. Hundreds of long ladders were lifted up. Many were cast down in ruin, but more replaced them, and Orcs sprang up them like apes in the dark forests of the South (II, 178).

The terror of nightmare lurks behind such descriptions as this. The massing of these unfeeling, brutalized, ines-

156

capable armies may not seem effective, in theory, but such descriptions work; carefully placed throughout *The Lord of the Rings*, such attacks by orcs—in Moria, in Helm's Deep, against the city of Minas Tirith—punctuate the individual and civilizing journeys of the Ringbearer or Gandalf or Aragorn, the lonely heroes working desperately to keep such hordes from taking over the earth. Like Shelob in her lair, the orcs depict the impersonal world of destruction and death which is the other side of man's self-awareness: the sense of being destroyed without reason, to lose control in some arbitrary and careless moment. The effect Tolkien achieves is something of the power we accord to our enemies; faceless, nameless, they are hordes engulfing our individual selves. One of our basic fears is that of being unable to argue with the maniac whom we cannot convince of our own worth and distinction. Tolkien also captures this in the swing of the Ringwraiths over the world, messengers of Sauron who are perfect for their purpose because they respond mechanically. Their flight across the marshes before the gates of Mordor captures the sense of horror in the ominous or inevitable.

The orcs are also frightening because of the world in which they live, the hideous dead environment of Mordor where nature has been perverted by Sauron into a desert of black rock, volcanoes, and camps of orcs and the slaves who serve this world. These are images drawn from traditional depictions of Hell, where the terrain in which the damned live reflects their natures. Sauron lives in a tower, Barad-dûr, which is isolated from the world. His creatures live in country equally bleak and unimaginatively inorganic:

> they went on up the ravine, until it ended in a sharp slope of screes and sliding stones. There the last living things gave up their struggle; the tops of the Morgai were grassless, bare, jagged, barren as a slate. . . . all seemed ruinous and dead, a desert burned and choked . . .
> (III, 244–5).

This is not only Hell; it is also the Desert of Temptation where the journeying soul is invited to despair. It is Tolkien's vision of the natural world perverted by the spread of factory and ghetto, of the industrial and urban ugliness of mankind seen in the author's own industrial cities, in the urban sprawl of America which shares the inhuman, inorganic sense of life mechanized and deadened.

For what is missing from the mind which separates itself from the community of fellow creatures, with Nature, is imagination. And, as we might expect in Tolkien, the language of the orcs reflects their inability to imagine and to love. The "Black Speech" of Barad-dûr was devised by Sauron for his servants; it is crude, coarse, unmusical, unpoetical. They have names like Gorbag and Snaga, and the language itself reflects their natures:

Ash nazg durbatuluk, as nazg gimbatul, ash nazg thrakataluk agh burzum-ishi krimputul!

When we compare this line in the Black Speech with that of the elves—"Arwen vanimelda, namarie!" for instance—with its liquid vowel sounds, the flowing of the line itself, we can see the difference. The Black Speech is a language for giving brutal orders, the tongue of the concentration camp and the slave ship. Tolkien illustrates the connection between nature and language morally: elves and dwarves, Aragorn and Gandalf "revered what was ancient, in language no less than in other matters, and they took pleasure in it according to their knowledge" (III, 514). To speak with care, to define exactly what is thought or felt, is a purposive imaginative act. But

Orcs and Trolls spoke as they would, without love of words or things; and their language was actually more degraded and filthy than I have shown it. I do not suppose that any will wish for a closer rendering, though models are easy to find. Much the same sort of talk can still be heard among the orc-minded; dreary and repetitive with hatred and contempt, too long removed from good to retain even verbal vigour, save in the ears of those to whom only the squalid sounds strong (III, 514).

To speak "as one would" without rules, definition, order, is to throw aside control over the image of oneself and over the imaginative relationship one has with the world, to care nothing for the shaping of words (or one's world) in a manner which is beautiful because it is complex, subtle, metaphoric and visionary of the relationship of mind and world. Beings who do not participate in the making of their world, who do not create a Secondary World, are not able to think well of themselves. Language reflects one's "degraded and filthy" condition. The creatures of Sauron do not have any songs, any poetry; they have no wish to know or to love other living things, to transcend themselves, to know the past.

Finally, there is the Gollum, Smeagol, who was not a creation of Sauron but becomes his creature through his passion for the One Ring, his "Precious." Smeagol is a living, horrible example of the destructive power of the Ring when it completely dominates the will of its victim-possessor, and Smeagol's language is a reflection of his enslaved condition. He illustrates on the one hand the self-destructive potential of all existing creatures in their desire for power. On the other, he shows how all beings somehow contribute, even against their wills, to the ultimate purposes of the universe. Thematically, the Gollum is important in *The Lord of the Rings* because he defines the alternative movement toward evil and self-destruction threatening Frodo; and because he "demands" from the hobbits pity and mercy, concomitants of power often lacking in other beings.

Smeagol, in fact, provides a parodic view of the history of the struggle for the One Ring, parodic in that his being and his motives are caricatures of others. But at the same time, the attitude of others toward him provides a standard by which they may be judged. He is both a scapegoat figure and, like Caliban in *The Tempest*, a test of the "humanity" of others. He is closer to Frodo than either would admit, being a distant hobbit relation, "clever-handed and quiet-footed" (I, 84). But where most hobbits fear the water and live a pastoral life, the Gollum loves the water and gives up living above ground, going instead to the roots of the mountains where Bilbo runs into him on his journey to the east: "his head and his eyes were downward." The Gollum's relationship to Nature is perverted, and an indication of his character. In a struggle for the One Ring, he kills his friend Deagol, much as Cain kills his brother Abel, because he wants it, without regard for the other. Neither Frodo nor Bilbo sought the Ring; it came to them. Smeagol takes it by design (or thinks he does), and uses it for malicious purposes until his people force him into the wilderness. For, as with all its "owners," the Ring "had given him power according to his nature." He uses the Ring to harm others, and finally to protect his consequent withdrawal into isolation and fear. The world he hoped to find under the mountains turns out to be worthless: "There was nothing more to find out, nothing worth doing, only nasty furtive eating and furtive remembering." He is the small selfish being turned in upon itself, feeding on its own stuff and discovering how little nutrition there is in such a meal.

And so with the larger theme of the Fellowship and the Quest. Smeagol goes alone after the Ring which Bilbo successfully captures from him in their riddle contest, and where Frodo feels the pull of the Ring and seeks its destruction, the Gollum is swallowed up by it. He cannot let it go. "He hated it and loved it, as he hated and loved himself. He could not get rid of it. He had no will left in the matter." And his Quest becomes not one for freedom, but for subjugation to the Precious again. The parody of larger minds comes out in his sense of what he has done. The murder of Deagol haunts him, and "he had made up a defense, repeating it" to himself, about how his grandmother had given him the ring for his birthday, because he *should* have gotten it for his birthday, as he saw the issue. Here is a parody on imaginative thinking: turning selfish wishing-it-were-true into reality: "It *was*

160

his birthday." This containment of the world in the image of himself is beautifully captured in Smeagol's language, which has dropped back from whatever it may have been, into the childish and barbaric patter of unsyntactical dialect, solipsistic like its source. He calls the lost Ring his "Precious," but he will often address himself and others in this form, identifying the world with his dream. He speaks with excessive sibilants to suggest the reptile nature he approaches in his depravity. His use of the plural first person pronoun when speaking of himself is a sign of his isolation. His confusion about himself and reality is beautifully, and painfully, captured as he climbs down a rock wall in the dark after Sam and Frodo:

> "Ach, sss! Cautious, my precious! More haste less speed. We musstn't rissk our neck, musst we, precious? No, precious—*gollum*!" He lifted his head again, blinked at the moon, and quickly shut his eyes. "We hate it," he hissed. "Nassty, nassty shivery light it is—sss-it spies on us, precious—it hurts our eyes." "Where iss it, where iss it: my precious, my precious? It's ours, it is, and we wants it" (II, 279).

This is not merely cute. It is the language of the frightened being as well as the compulsive; speech is used as a defense against the world instead of a way of experiencing it. And here of course, Smeagol's fear of the moon and its light is a rejection of Nature which for others, cheers and heals.

In ironic counterpoint to the others, Smeagol has no sense of the plan of the universe working itself out in history and willed endeavor; he sees himself and his pain within this narrow sphere, "animal" not only in his form but in the range of his imagination. And so where the Quest opens up new worlds to the hobbits, and their vision changes and expands to meet these new worlds, for Smeagol the journey is merely a repetition of his miserable vision of life, whining and crouching, hurt by the elven rope about his ankle, licking Frodo's feet, and then betraying him to Shelob: the world as enemy. The Gollum is not only at the bottom of the scale of creatures in *The Lord of the Rings*; he is that failure of perception which Tolkien describes in "On Fairy-Stories" as the failure of Recovery, to regain "a clear view" of things "apart from ourselves." Smeagol never does this, even after Frodo befriends him. Tolkien is thus relying on Smeagol's "history" in that he is very much physically and imaginatively as he appears in *The Hobbit* where Bilbo encounters him: "as dark as darkness, save for two big round pale eyes in his thin face." But he serves larger purposes in the Trilogy where he provides Frodo with a kind of alter-ego. He is to be pitied for the misery which he has brought on himself in pursuit of the Ring, and Tolkien shows the Gollum with the possibility of reform, arguing with himself about whether to try to destroy Frodo before he can destroy the Precious, a schizophrenic debate in which the one voice records Frodo's kindness, and the other demands the Ring: "We wants it!" (II, 303–5) The "good" half loses, but at least the inner debate does take place, and its real point in the fantasy is to parallel Frodo's own inner struggle, where a similar debate between will and inclination goes on. Frodo makes the captured Gollum swear to help the hobbits to Mordor, making him swear by the One Ring.

> "No! not on it," said Frodo, looking down at him with stern pity. "All you wish is to see it and touch it, if you can, though you know it would drive you mad. Not on it. Swear by it, if you will. For you know where it is. Yes, you know, Smeagol. It is before you."
>
> For a moment it appeared to Sam that his master had grown and Gollum had shrunk: a tall stern shadow, a mighty lord who hid his brightness in grey cloud, and at his feet a little whining dog. Yet the two were in some way akin and not alien: they could reach one another's minds (II, 285).

They are "akin" because both can be tempted by power beyond their natures; they are both available for the

162

degradation of possession and the consequent failure to achieve Recovery. Frodo can see in Smeagol what he himself might have been. Sam's vision of Frodo as a mighty lord is of one who is still in control of himself, through his will, as Smeagol is not, but who can still transcend his own personal suffering in the horrors of the Quest, and feel pity and grant mercy for a fellow-sufferer. For Frodo remembers what Gandalf had said long ago in the Shire about the possible values of showing mercy to the Gollum, and it is one of Tolkien's successes that he makes this paradox live as an important one in the fantasy. Frodo is both above the Gollum and a sufferer like him. In his own spiritual struggle he acknowledges other created beings, not just by "seeing" them but by "feeling" for them, too, and thus respecting their dignity, their individuality, however much it may be lost to them.

Structually, the Gollum is important because his desperation for the Ring leads him to destroy it himself by struggling for it on the brink of the Cracks of Doom and falling in at the very moment of possession. His destruction, while the others live, is the final irony in his petty, vital career. But Tolkien's invention of the Gollum was essential; an alternative view to that of the hobbits is necessary, to show what they might have become. And Smeagol's small size, his smallness of vision—and his being "imagined" in a moral as well as a perceptual sense by Frodo (and Tolkien)—are illustrative of another kind of fear than that fostered by the orcs in their massed phalanxes. Smeagol is the desperation within us, the lack of an imagined self—as opposed to the threat from without which orcs represent. No greater evidence is needed of Tolkien's increasingly complex perception in his career as a fantasist, than his change in villain from the simply conceived (and borrowed) Smaug of *The Hobbit* to the rather more complex (and imagined) victim, the Gollum, in *The Lord of the Rings*.

This wide-ranging selection of characters, representative of different races, of the past and the present, of different imaginative capacity and point of view is designed by

Tolkien to show the wide variety of life in Middle-earth. Such variety must be respected, not reduced to conform to a dominant will. Furthermore, each race and each member of that race must assume the responsibility for the support of civilization in Middle-earth to the extent of his power. The figures like elves and dwarves drawn from the history of the Third Age, and figures like ents and hobbits imagined by Tolkien, cover the spectrum of imaginative life in the world and also make history meaningful by their participation in it. A struggle for power is inevitable, as time runs downward to its end, but individual beings participate in the decisions which direct the historical struggle this way or that. History is not just the inevitable working out of time in ways beyond the imagination's power. What we also see in this range of characters is a hierarchical ranking depending upon what they can do with the particular abilities at their disposal. And heroism is in turn a complex element in a world determined by choice. Aragorn needs support from men and hobbits, wizards and elves to attain his destined kingship. Frodo needs Aragorn and all the others, including Smeagol and Smaug the dragon from his Uncle Bilbo's Quest, if he is to succeed. Beowulf fought monsters single-handed; in the Secondary World of Middle-earth, which is more like our Primary World than Beowulf's Land of the Danes, the necessary interdependence of created beings who must often fight with swords but more often with their imaginations makes a simplified map of the battlefield between good and evil impossible.

It is true that in the last analysis, Tolkien's characters do not have the deeply explored complexity of motivation which we associate with modern psychological and historical novels. Only in the rare case of Frodo and perhaps Sam Gamgee does Tolkien approximate the kind of character development which we know from realistic fiction. In these figures, the complexity of the character's situation may increase as Frodo and Sam come to mean more and more to each other and to the effort against Sauron. But their motives are expressed in terms of easily discernible choices: to will, to endure, to be loyal. What Tolkien has abandoned (or, rather, subdued) is the *ambiguity* of choice and the effect of moral and imaginative judgments on character. The One Ring must be destroyed, and certain steps must be taken and not others. And so long as everyone understands that the good of the whole world community comes before the selfish end of power sought for its own sake, all decisions are really made on a fairly self-evident basis. Tolkien makes it very clear in "On Fairy-Stories" that certain essential values are always the end of imaginative experience: to talk to and respect other living beings, for instance, or to discover "the inner consistency of reality." Excessive pride in one's power is wrong. But fantasy reveals the "inner reality" through the creation of the Secondary World, and consequently, Tolkien strives not for the realism of presentation which we associate with the novel, but for the symbolic representation of moral reality through images, through poetic speech and action committed exactly because the motives for action, hidden though they may often be, are not ambiguous or unavailable. Tolkien's link between fantasy and the imagination is important because in such representation the reader's imagination must assist in the creation of effective symbols which are ultimately moral in their implications, as opposed to the psychological validity sought by the novelist who is more concerned with causes that *drive* the character rather than ends that *lead* him on through choice. Fantasy thus requires characters who are psychologically relatively simple; the values for which they stand are clear and self-evident to the imaginative eye and the character's task is to represent them as well as to seek them out. As Blake long ago pointed out, perception and morality are the same thing in both the Primary and Secondary Worlds.

Chapter Six:

Patterns: The Growth of a Legend

When all is said and done, we are less interested in the characters in *The Lord of the Rings* for what they are than for what they do. The One Ring is successfully destroyed; Sauron's power is overthrown; Aragorn returns to the throne of his fathers, and the War of the Ring initiates the age in which we now live, the Age of Men. We must try to explain why these events are so important to readers of the Trilogy, first in terms of how Tolkien the Enchanter and Historian encourages Secondary Belief in his fantasy; and second, in terms of the values which underlie the characters' journeys to the end of an era. The Enchanter's power to create a believable

Secondary World is essential if he is to convince his readers of the value of imagination in the Primary World. The Third Age ends not only because the time has come, according to the plans of the universe, but also because men and hobbits, a wizard, some elves and others unite to assert good in the world. A new age begins, and it is the task of created beings to order it for the better. As Gandalf explains, the Allies against Sauron must do "what is in us for the succour of those years wherein we are set, uprooting the evil in the fields that we know, so that those who live after may have clean earth to till" (III, 190). So at the end of the Trilogy, with Sauron gone and Paradise regained, we have some kind of answer to the difficult question: What can a man do to be saved, in the Primary World? A question often asked by mortal men who feel powerless to act as individual beings, or to do any good thing against the seemingly unbeatable forces of evil. If Tolkien is right and the imagination can operate in the Primary World as it does in the Secondary, then we can find an analogy for our life in *The Lord of the Rings*; we can also find answers to the crucial question of salvation. How is power to be used, dangerous to the user as it is? How does the individual created being fit into the plans of the universe we see in operation in the Trilogy?

One answer lies in the structure of the Secondary World as Tolkien imagines it. Our belief in the events that occur is sustained by the Enchanter's power of creating a convincing vision of experience in Middle-earth. The action that takes place there is essentially moral in that good triumphs over evil, and we see and feel that struggle and sacrifice transform not only history but the individual as well. The Trilogy is not just the record of events leading to Sauron's fall. It is also a statement about value which events and personalities illustrate, as they appear on the stages of the journey into the Fourth Age. The basic structural element is the Quest, but Tolkien has complicated its form by providing two complementary quests that seemingly move in opposed directions: Frodo's effort to destroy the One Ring, and Aragorn's assertion of his true self and his "return" to rule over Middle-earth. Both quests, however, destroy certain things and affirm or re-

167

construct certain things; and in the overall pattern made by the heroes on their journeys, both quests are necessary for the working out of history. Structurally, the quests provide a series of exciting events which hold our attention; together, they give us a sense of the epic scope of historical process as it spreads out over Middle-earth from the Shire to Gondor, in the air with eagles and Nazgûl, on the waters of Anduin, even underground in the mines of Moria.

Thematically, the quests show us the developing sense of self and of life which the heroes experience on their journeys. This is especially true in the case of Frodo, for while Aragorn is an important figure, we become much more interested in the hobbit's career. Partly this is because Tolkien gives us a rather distant and idealized picture of the future King Elessar from the beginning; we never see him making the agonized decisions Frodo must make, and he usually appears, not as a lonely wanderer in the wasteland, but as the leader and decision maker for a group of hobbits, men like the Dunédain, or the Allies in their final vast league against Sauron. More importantly, we see Frodo forced to make a number of decisions, uncertain of his will and physical strength to sustain them, as Aragorn is not. We see Frodo frequently valiant but helpless before an attack by the Black Riders or Shelob, often on the edge of disaster, and we want to know if he will survive. And, finally, as Roger Sale has pointed out, the major events of the quest are represented from the hobbit point of view.[18] Often Merry, Pippin or Sam Gamgee takes Frodo's place as observer of the action or commentator on it, but it is still the view of hobbits who leave the safe world of the Shire for a much more dangerous and uncertain one, and whose growth as heroic figures is connected with their increased perception of the deepest significance of events. Frodo is not only the suffering victim the Enemy must "get"; he is also the character whose inner growth is most important to Tolkien's imaginative perspective. In other words, the attraction of *The Lord of the Rings* for its readers lies in Tolkien's ability to create exciting events pertaining to the developing quest, and at the same time to give those events imaginative significance. We quickly become involved in what happens to Frodo or Gandalf, and this involvement represents the success of Tolkien's effort to create Secondary Belief. For, finally, what we have been describing has been the essentially religious nature of fantasy as Tolkien sees it, and Frodo and the other heroic figures of the Trilogy achieve an imaginative transcendence of experience by immersing themselves in experience, the Quest itself, and in such a way that we are convinced of their transformation.

Structurally, then, there is the panoramic view of Middle-earth and beyond, which opens up as the quests progress: the hobbits move eastward from the Shire with its familiar and protective sights into unknown country where race after race of unfamiliar beings appear until at last almost all of Middle-earth has become involved in the War of the Ring. This is not an internal battle, one fought within the individual soul, as in much modern literature. It involves everyone in the world, and this sense of vastness, of large areas and great deeds, is infectious. Tolkien epitomizes this epic perspective in Frodo's vision from atop Amon Hen where, seated in the chair of the ancient Guardian Kings of Gondor, he sees the world in upheaval under the threat of Sauron with orcs, men, elves, wolves in combat: "The land of the Beornings was aflame; a cloud was over Moria; smoke rose on the borders of Lórien" (I, 518). Although Tolkien presents a very general and grand picture as Frodo sees the world, he is careful to link the vision with the theme; on Amon Hen, Frodo also feels the Eye of Sauron seeking him, and he must decide whether to leave on the One Ring, which has given his hiding place away, or take it off and escape again from the Dark Lord.

Such scenes are rarely grand or exciting events for their own sake. Tolkien emphasizes the epic character of his picture by borrowing from traditional literary epic not only the combat of heroes in sword and armor, and the movement of armies across a vast landscape. He even begins *The Lord of the Rings in media res*, that is, in the middle of the action, a typical epic convention. Frodo's part in the Quest was initiated long before he and Gandalf discussed the Ring Bilbo left behind in the peaceful Shire. The forces of evil had been abroad long before, as *The Hobbit* and Gandalf's history of the Shadow of the Past record. And, of course, this sense of the stretch of time contributes to the import of great events. On the other hand, Tolkien initiates the action of his "epic" with a whimsical birthday-party for the old hobbit, Bilbo, not a traditional event in epic poetry. We may feel this is too playful a scene with its mindless hobbit families and Bilbo's trick of vanishing at the climax of the festivities. But Tolkien does this to suggest the ordinary character of hobbits, and how unsuited they are for the necessary heroics demanded of them. The point, of course, is that Frodo and Merry and Pippin and Sam *do* respond to the challenges of the Ring, and from the rather crudely satiric middle-class celebration of family and home, the action opens up unexpectedly into the brutal realities of Frodo's lonely quest, and the creation of a very different kind of "family," the Fellowship of the Ring.

Another structural element which sustains our attention is the way in which the action of the quest takes place, usually to put Frodo in peril of his life and save him in the nick of time; or to show him making a significant decision, the "choices" by which he exercises his freedom and his own nature as Frodo the Hobbit. Thus the Ring-bearer escapes eastward from the Black Riders on his trail by fleeing with his companions through the Old Forest. There, they are attacked by Old Willow and rescued by Tom Bombadil. On their way again, the hobbits are lost on the Barrow-downs and nearly become wraiths, like the inhabitants of the barrows, only to be rescued once again by Bombadil and set on the road to Bree. Again the Black Riders appear on their trail, follow them to Weathertop, and stab Frodo with a nearly fatal wound that remains painful for the rest of his life on Middle-earth. In the days that follow, and with the help of Aragorn under his disguise as the Ranger "Strider," the hobbits escape to Rivendell and the safety of Elrond's protection, Frodo just missing being captured once more at the Ford of the Longwater.

These escapes become increasingly tense, with a carefully built-up momentum of pursuit and last-moment flight, until at the Longwater Frodo is alone on his elven horse, a jump ahead of the Black Riders. He is carried through the river, but the Riders are close behind him and when they enter the water, a flood sweeps the Black Riders away, though not forever, for they proceed through a series of transformations to become the Nazgûl. Frodo escapes once again through luck, endurance and the aid of his friends. The quest at this stage is less the search for great ends than a melodrama of pursuit and escape. But Tolkien has been careful to modify this basic pattern in several ways. In the first place, the history of the Ring-bearer is coordinated by a series of "councils" in which the adventurers discuss what steps to take. Gandalf, for instance, tells Frodo the story of the Ring, tells him that he has evidently been chosen to guard it, for the moment at least, and suggests that it must be thrown into the Cracks of Doom. Such councils are repeated throughout the initial journey to Rivendell. But Strider or Gandalf or Sam provide counsel only; they do not command Frodo, who must bear the responsibility of deciding what to do with the Ring himself. He decides to go away from the Shire in order to save it, the first in a series of personal sacrifices for the good of the community. More importantly, perhaps, Frodo makes his own decisions and acts upon them. The "conferences," which culminate in the Great Council of Elrond in Rivendell, are thematically important because they show the wise and the good offering what they can to the Ring-bearer, in a civilized act of discussion. Such conferences illustrate the respect members of the world community show each other and confirming the respect to be shown individuals, as opposed to the authoritarian ruthlessness of Sauron or his creatures. Thus the moments of action when Frodo is in flight are initiated by discussions: in the world of Tolkien, decisions are followed by events in the Secondary World (even if the action is only "running scared"). Tolkien keeps the suspense up with action which is fast-paced and exciting but which is based upon imaginatively-important decisions.

In other words, as readers we are asked to meet hobbits

171

whom we have not known existed, and then to recognize that for all their seeming uniqueness, hobbits are enough like human beings to make us feel that their presence in *The Lord of the Rings* is important. We then become involved with Frodo, his flight from the Shire and his decision to destroy the One Ring. Our perspective on this world is altered enough by the presence of hobbits to demand that imagination come into play. We worry about the Ring-bearer, and his ability to escape the Enemy and get to Rivendell. And this concentration on adventure involves us for more important things later on. The journey to Mordor is matched with an interior journey reflecting Frodo's development through the demands made upon him by the Quest. In the flight from the Shire to Rivendell, Frodo is helpless before his enemies, but he shows the necessary endurance to survive. He is also surrounded by other hobbits, a protective band forming the prototype for the Fellowship of the Ring. And in the course of the journey south with the Ring, we see Frodo grow increasingly alone, less dependent upon aid from others. Thus he leaves the protective Shire where innocence of the world has kept hobbits secure if unaware. At Bree, "Strider" joins the hobbits as a guide, but at Rivendell Frodo learns that this Ranger is really a prince in disguise, and while the shock is a welcome one, it reveals to the hobbit that much is hidden in the world. Later in Moria, Gandalf is lost, and at the end of their journey down the Anduin, Boromir breaks his vow of loyalty, is killed by orcs, and the Fellowship itself dissolves as Frodo determines to continue alone with the One Ring. The journey to the end of Book I, in other words, explores new country and identifies many of the allies, like dwarves and elves, who will join against the Dark Lord.

But Frodo not only loses helpful companions; he also loses his protective sense of reality. Frodo begins his career as Ring-bearer in the Shire where he was "chosen" for what he *is*: "not for power or wisdom, at any rate," says Gandalf, but for reasons not yet clear in the cosmic scheme (I, 95). We learn later that hobbit endurance and hobbit obscurity as a race unknown to Sauron played

172

a part in the selection. But, as the journey goes forward, Frodo becomes more important for what he *does*: for instance, when the hobbits are trapped in the barrow-grave, it is he who stabs the threatening hand with a sword and remembers the song calling Tom Bombadil to their rescue. At the Council of Elrond he makes a different kind of decision: to take the Ring to Mordor since it seems to be his responsibility. Later, in the progress of the Fellowship south, he is carried along (at times, literally) by Gandalf and Strider; his small sword, Sting, is good in a pinch, but not much help against a Balrog. But on Amon Hen, after he has been threatened by the Eye, and has seen that even the Fellowship can be subverted by the desire for power, he decides to go on alone. The task is his, and he wishes to save the members of the Company, whom he loves.

This decision splits the Company, which would seem disastrous, but it initiates a necessary division of strength, for Frodo, joined by the loyal Sam, goes on to Mordor, and Strider-Aragorn leads a diversion west, a movement which leads to the rescue of Gondor and keeps Sauron busy so that Frodo can slip through his guard. Frodo's decision is important at the thematic level, since it represents a sacrifice for the good of others, a heroic choice to give up the comfort of companionship for the uncertainty of self-reliance. It is the end of a sequence in which Frodo's defenses against the world have dropped away, forcing him to fall back upon himself. Our interest is held here, as it is all along the Quest, by the question of what will happen to the Ring-bearer in his struggle to preserve his freedom. The Ring calls him constantly to give in to it, to accept the peace offered by surrender to a greater Will. Before Weathertop, he puts on the Ring when threatened by the Black Riders, thereby revealing himself to them: "Not with the hope of escape, or of doing anything, either good or bad: he simply felt that he must take the Ring and put it on his finger," even though Gandalf has warned him not to (I, 262). It is then that he receives the wound marking him as a scapegoat, a sacred sacrifice for the community. The Ring begins to make increasing demands on his will. Later, escaped to

Lorien, Frodo looks into the Mirror of Galadriel, feels the power of the Eye searching for him, and the tug of his burden: "The Ring that hung upon its chain about his neck grew heavy, heavier than a great stone" (I, 471), and it nearly draws him into the water of the Mirror. Galadriel, by contrast, keeps her mind firm against Sauron, and the "door" by which the Dark Lord might enter, remains closed. It is Frodo who must bear the burden of almost continual choice, weak as he is. Hence the significance of his decision on Amon Hen. There, putting on the Ring and so accepting its power, he feels the Eye on him, and hears Gandalf's ethereal but commonsense command: *"Take it off! Fool, take it off! Take off the Ring!"*

> The two powers strove in him. For a moment, perfectly balanced between their piercing points, he writhed, tormented. Suddenly he was aware of himself again. Frodo, neither the Voice nor the Eye: free to choose, and with one remaining instant in which to do so. He took the Ring off his finger (I, 519).

This active assertion of himself saves him: "A great weariness was on him, but his will was firm and his heart lighter." He then puts the Ring on in order to escape from the Company and their aid, but this is a necessary sacrifice based on his own understanding of himself and what he must do. At such points in the narrative, Frodo's internal struggle becomes more important than external events, and we hang on his decision because its consequence tells us what the Ring-bearer has become under the pressure of his burden. Tolkien is expert at this suspenseful drawing-out of Frodo's powers, and this sense of Frodo's development under temptation to be more than he is creates the fantasy's effect beyond others in its class. We do not find such tension in *The Hobbit*, nor the "moral seriousness" associated with decision-making. The Ring "stretches" the soul until it passes invisible barriers into the realm of the Dark Lord; Frodo's decision to meet this challenge and to accept the suffering it must entail is a moving culmination of his initiation into the world of experience.

Tolkien is also careful to illustrate Frodo's development on the Quest through his perception of the world and of himself. The Trilogy is consistently narrated from the hobbits' point of view, which, of course, changes as they move out of the familiar Shire into the unknown. Under such conditions, perception becomes a moral quality defining reality and inviting our participation in the development Frodo undergoes. Frodo learns from Gandalf that the world is not as it seems: The old ring Bilbo left him is *the* One Ring sought by Sauron; the Shire has enemies that threaten its peaceful and self-satisfied isolation. Tolkien also uses moments of vision like that on the barrow-downs when the hobbits foresee the coming of King Alessar with "a star on his brow." But it is usually concrete description from their position, Frodo or Sam looking about a room or seeing the threatening mass of the Old Forest where "there was not as yet any sign of a path, and the trees seemed constantly to bar their way." Strider-Aragorn appears to us through their eyes, so that his unmasking of his true self to them is a surprise to us as well. Again, the threat posed by the Black Riders at Weathertop is told from the hobbits' view, as the black figures run toward them, seemingly inescapable. When Frodo puts on the Ring, and the evil beings appear for what they are, "beneath their black wrappings," they take on mythic qualities, robed in grey with helms of silver, one crowned: kings of death seen only in their true form by the wearer of the Ring. Frodo's view often defines for us the interchangeable area between vision and reality in this Secondary World. Furthermore, the wound he receives from the visionary king of the dead begins to change him, too, so that he notices that he can see better in the dark than his companions; his increased ability to feel, however, increases the weight of the Ring.

At the same time, Frodo's growing awareness has its compensations in his perception of the reality of life beyond what he had known. Thus his first view of Lorien stops him "in wonder": "a light was upon it for which his

175

language had no name." The shapes and colors of the trees and flowers are familiar but "fresh and poignant, as if he had at that moment first perceived them and made for them names new and wonderful." "Wonder" takes real physical form in the elven woodland, but it is Frodo's availability for wonder, as well: "never before had he been so suddenly and so keenly aware of the feel and texture of a tree's skin and of the life within it. He felt a delight in wood and the touch of it, neither as forester nor as carpenter; it was the delight of the living tree itself" (I, 454–5). To feel this "delight" in the tree is to feel it in himself as well, to imagine "wonder" through communication with other living things. The vision of a higher and better world on which, like Lórien, there is "no stain," is realizable by hobbits and men. And vision is not just visual but *feeling*, for part of Frodo's response to the "delight" in a tree's life is in his felt response. This vision leads, in turn, to a view of Aragorn transcendent, "wrapped in some fair memory: and as Frodo looked at him he knew that he beheld things as they once had been in this same place. For the grim years were removed from the face of Aragorn, and he seemed clothed in white, a young lord tall and fair: and he spoke words in the Elvish tongue to one whom Frodo could not see. *Arwen vanimelda, namarie!*" (I, 456). The beauty of a passage like this, describing men and trees in the woods of Lórien, lies in the multi-layered richness of the experience: in Frodo's sense of release, for the moment, from the trials of the Ring; in his awareness of a wonderful new world and his place in it; in his sudden sense of the visible present fulfilling a rich and timeless past in the person of a man he has come to love. The "light" in Aragorn's eyes is that of "some fair memory" and so is the light of "the moral power of goodness" which ennobles those who can receive it. [19] This is an *epiphany*, a moment of perception when the natural world and the divine appear as one, both to Aragorn and to the wondering Frodo, but it is a vision which is the product of Frodo's past experience in the world in its multi-leveled and concrete variety. At the same time, it takes a small creature like Frodo to bring

176

all these elements into harmony. Or rather, ironically, it takes the perverse power of the Ring he carries.

For we cannot forget the alternative to Frodo's self-sacrifice: the Fellowship of the Ring, and its growth into the Allies united against Sauron. At a time when the good on Middle-earth are threatened by the loss of their individual freedom, the hierarchy of creatures, each race with its special powers, must be united to defend the Community. The Fellowship constituted by Elrond to accompany Frodo to the south requires that its members work together for the common good, "identifying" with each other, rather than emphasizing their differences. [20] In this way they contribute without being subordinate to another. Tolkien sets up a history of warfare between elves and dwarves which the friendship of Gimli and Legolas, developed through their journeys together, modifies. But Legolas can see further than others with his elven vision, can run over the snow without sinking in; Gimli can delight in the treasures beneath the earth, and fight with an axe. Again, the hobbits, Merry and Pippin, also rise to larger purposes: they begin the Quest through the excitement of the adventure, a desire to help Frodo, jealousy of Sam who is admitted to the Fellowship before them. But they achieve selflessness when Merry enters the service of King Theoden, Pippin that of Denethor, deliberate acts of allegiance which become important: Merry, for instance, is on hand to help Eowyn destroy the Nazgûl.

Such service is based not upon the self-elevating actions of a hero like Beowulf, but upon love given to others. Both Gandalf and Aragorn show their power *and* their love toward the members of the Fellowship and especially toward the hobbits on the journeys they share: carrying them, humoring them. Gandalf literally sacrifices himself in the Mines of Moria; Aragorn finds king's foil, the herb of healing, to place on Frodo's wound, and decides to go in pursuit of the hobbits captured by orcs, rather than to follow Frodo into the wilderness: ". . . if I seek him now . . ., I must abandon the captives to torment and death. My heart speaks clearly at last: the fate of the Bearer is in my hands no longer. . . . Yet we that remain cannot forsake our companions while we have strength left" (II, 26). Such selfless commitment is not possible to the creatures of the Enemy, who live in fear of one another, as the constant strife among the orcs illustrates. The Fellowship is held together by ties of loyalty based upon deep affection, rather than upon oaths or self-aggrandizement. This turns inside out the historic definition of the *comitatus*, the band of loyal retainers accompanying a hero in history and myth, a band usually dependent, as in *Beowulf*, upon their lord's prowess and prestige and upon his gifts of gold. And certainly this is a different group than that of the dwarves who go with the "burglar," Bilbo, to regain their hoarded treasures in *The Hobbit*. The service of love in the Fellowship, with its quasi-feudal trappings of swords and oaths, provides its members with a sense of unified purpose in which they can believe, a community effort to which they can contribute because of what they are as individuals. The most important element in this Fellowship is the sense of meaning in the world which members can believe in and act upon. Within the Secondary World of the Trilogy, strong feelings, deep commitment, are possible, a response to the potentially tragic crisis of the Ring. Such feeling, stronger than sexual passion, transcends sexuality exactly as the good of the community must be put above that of the individual. The historical pattern Tolkien follows here could be that provided by the English experience in World War II, in which men seemed united throughout the world against a terrible, overwhelming enemy. One of the things which makes Tolkien's fantasy so moving is this sense of impending apocalypse, and the response of created beings to it.

The Fellowship and the alliance against Sauron that grows out of it serve both structural and thematic purposes. We must also say that the history of the gathering armies in the west; the adventures of Aragorn with the Rohirrim and the army of the Dead; even the thrilling convergence of friend and enemy on the battlefield before Minas Tirith—these are adventures less important to us as discoverers of the Secondary World than Frodo and Sam's life under the Eye of Sauron. This is inevitable, given

Tolkien's emphasis upon Frodo's struggle and the character of the history he records. Aragorn must grow in the exercise of his strength, and bring to final recognition his essential nature as the mythic king, the political and spiritual symbol of a united world. But we never see him forced to suffer in those wastelands of the spirit where Frodo wanders. His decisions are those of the future king, and so we never see his internal struggle, if there is one, as we see Frodo's who is closer to being "human" in this existential sense than King Elessar. The excitement in this next phrase of *The Lord of the Rings* lies in the timing of events, when Gandalf must ride Shadowfax through the night to reach Minas Tirith, or when the Rohirrim finally arrive as Gandalf confronts the Lord of the Nazgûl at the city's very gate. There is excitement, too, in the battles, the hand-to-hand combat, the arrival of Aragorn with the fleet from the south, but we have moved into a period when the conventions of romance—the battles, the sentimental love affair, the ride to save the worthy—do not touch our imaginations as deeply as do Frodo and Sam. Battles with death and destruction are necessary; evil takes physical form in order to be dealt with by the imagination, and so it is natural that the Quest should seem to terminate in a battle between good and evil, as it does even in such Christian epics as Milton's *Paradise Lost*. But the greater exercise of the imagination occurs in Merry's wounding of the Nazgûl, in Gandalf's attempt to outguess Sauron, encouraging the Dark Lord to send out his armies so that the Ring-bearer may get through undetected: "We must walk open-eyed into that trap, with courage, but small hope for ourselves. . . . But this, I deem, is our duty. And better so than to perish nonetheless—as we surely shall, if we sit here—and know as we die that no new age shall be" (III,191–2). This is the moral vision that transcends any other.

For the Apocalypse, in which the world is destroyed in order to be renewed, occurs not through the power of captains or kings, but through the will of the diminutive Ring-bearer. His is a lonely journey whose consequences he does not even know; the black wasteland through which he travels is the physical equivalent of his despair as it is the expression of Sauron's destructive power. But the relationship which he develops with Sam, on the other hand, is a "fellowship" expressive of the greater power of the moral vision based upon imagination. The hero and a servant-friend go back a long way in western literature, back through Huckleberry Finn and Jim floating down the Mississippi to European antecedents whose most famous examplars are Don Quixote and Sancho Panza. But by placing Frodo and Sam in the wasteland of Mordor —lonely, near despair, but together—Tolkien has cast them in the most contemporaneous of roles: that of outcasts who nevertheless can believe in each other and so form their own supportive society. In Beckett's *Waiting for Godot*, the two tramps wait for Godot, who never comes, in a nearly empty setting, but they wait *together*, giving each other support which the external world does not provide. Tolkien successfully juxtaposes this modern vision of man's paradoxical aloneness and dependency against the dramatic background of the traditional romance view of heroism in an ordered world. Frodo and Sam's mutual dependency creates a small community, a "little world" in which they may survive destruction. They, too, must "wait together" and Frodo's determination, which at times nearly succumbs to despair or to his passion for the Ring, is sustained by the loving presence of Sam as well as by his own stubbornness. This friendship, developed through necessity in the wastes of Mordor, is the culmination of Tolkien's vision, where the imagination is put to the test as a force for man's salvation.

For, most importantly, Sam and Frodo *believe* in each other and exchange that mutual trust that is respect and love for other living things. The world of the Quest is now viewed exclusively from hobbit-level, and it is horrible, hurting the body and destructive to the spirit, just as it is symbolic of the death-wishing mind that made it a prison for the imagination. Thus in the wastes of the Emyn Muil the storm is accompanied by the screams of a Nazgûl, repeated later in the Dead Marshes, a constant reminder of Sauron's pursuit, as is the "naked waste" itself. The repetition of such scenes and sounds, as the hobbits know them, carries to us "that horrible growing sense of a hostile will that strove with great power to pierce all shadows of cloud, and earth, and flesh, and to see you: to pin you under its deadly gaze, naked, immovable. So thin, so frail and thin, the veils were become that still warded it off" (II, 301). In the Dead Marshes the faces of warriors from the past stare back at the travelers: "all foul, all rotting, all dead" (II,297)—all seen by Frodo, and they are the symbolic equivalent of his own tempting despair. We also know it is the world of industrial waste, of the natural world utterly ruined by that "possessiveness" which drains it for profit, without care for its destruction: "a land defiled, diseased beyond all healing—unless the Great Sea should enter in and wash it with oblivion" (II, 302). Observed through Frodo's eyes, this dead world of the potential future is saved from being merely allegorical. The "gasping pools" choked "with ash and crawling muds," the "high mounds of crushed and powdered rock, great cones of earth fire-blasted and poison-stained," appear like "an obscene graveyard" where even the light of the morning is "reluctant" to show itself (II, 302). Only creatures with feelings who are "reluctant" to enter this desert could read the light as "reluctant" and give some kind of life to this world.

Tolkien is careful to increase the tension which Frodo feels in himself over the pull of the Ring. The Eye and its barren world can overcome Frodo only if he lets it; if his will is strong enough, he will survive. But we must observe the tension. As the Ring-bearer comes slowly closer to the inner fortress of Sauron, the temptation to give up becomes greater. At times Frodo even questions the value of free will when both alternatives in a choice seem equally destructive: "Which way should he choose? And if both led to terror and death, what good lay in choice?" (II, 319). At other times, he is not even conscious of his self deciding his fate, but simply gives in. Again and again, "as if some force were at work other than his own will," he turns toward the Dark Lord, "his sense reeling and his mind darkening." Sam, who is not touched by the power of the Ring, can pull him back. But the escape is often a narrow one:

181

The luminous tower fascinated him, and he fought the desire that was on him to run up the gleaming road towards its gate. At last with an effort he turned back, and as he did so, he felt the Ring resisting him, dragging at the chain about his neck; and his eyes too, as he looked away, seemed for the moment to have been blinded. The darkness before him was impenetrable (II, 398).

Frodo can even turn against Sam at a moment when he most needs him, so caught up is he in the toils of the Ring. Sam has carried the Ring for a time, and when he offers to continue carrying it, Frodo snatches it back.

"No you won't, you thief!" he panted, staring at Sam with eyes wide with fear and enmity. Then suddenly, clasping the Ring in one clenched fist, he stood aghast. A mist seemed to clear from his eyes, and he passed a hand over his aching brow. The hideous vision had seemed so real to him, half bemused as he was still with wound and fear. Sam had changed before his very eyes into an orc again, leering and pawing at his treasure, a foul little creature with greedy eyes and slobbering mouth. But now the vision had passed (III, 230).

The connection between perception and moral vision is very clear in this passage: the imagination falters and Frodo, for a moment, can only see Sam as he is himself, anxious to possess the Ring and to be possessed. It renders him "inhuman," distorting his vision so that the beauty of Sam's loving nature takes the form of an ugly orc, and identifies Frodo, for a moment, with the wasted landscape, the revolting slaves of Sauron, the Eye of the Dark Lord. Frodo's vision clears; he can be "blinded"—he can become like the world of Mordor he sees—but he is also still available to love, to the goodness which still lives in his hobbit-nature. When the passage of the Wraithlord from the gates of Mordor tempts him into giving up, he touches the phial of Galadriel: "all thought of the Ring was banished from his mind," and the terrible figure turns away, Frodo's mind, strengthened for the moment, holding him off (II, 401). And so with this vision of Sam, who reappears to the blinded Frodo "kneeling before him, his face wrung with pain, as if he had been stabbed in the heart; tears welled from his eyes" (III, 230). And Frodo is a hobbit again. Frodo is available for both love and hate, freedom and imprisonment. This complexity keeps him from becoming merely the fairy-story figure who is never tempted by his own desires. His greatest heroism is in his final desperate ability to remain true to his nature: like all Quests, this journey is a "stretching," a *test* of the limits of personality as the moral vision represents it.

But created beings, in Tolkien's world do not, need not, survive alone. Sam Gamgee, who goes with Frodo to the Cracks of Doom, is his aid and comforter; Gollum, who accompanies them, for better or worse, is Frodo's "dark" side, the depraved outcast and slave to the Ring. When Frodo can at times do nothing more for himself in this wilderness, one or the other help him out. For Sam this is simply "hobbit-sense" and a deep love for his "master," Mr. Frodo. For Smeagol the journey is one of pain because he will finally lose the "Precious" to either the Dark Lord or to the Cracks of Doom, as Frodo moves slowly closer to his goal. But he also makes an effort to help Frodo, the Ring's "master," and to feel, briefly, some hint of the love or friendship which is the concomitant of the moral imagination. Both Sam and Smeagol are necessary to complete the Quest.

Like the other questers, Sam, too, is tested, but he cannot really go to the limits as Frodo can. He begins as the gardener's son whose closeness to Nature and simple capacity for devotion seem to keep him safe. It is possible to complain that Tolkien has set up a classic master-servant relationship here, with a certain English snobbishness built into it; but working with just such a long literary tradition—the hero who searches and dreams, the loyal retainer who saves him with common sense in a pinch—Tolkien is also presenting a certain kind of elemental "human" nature: steadfast loyalty which cannot be corrupted. Sam carries the rope for rescuing Frodo from the cliffs; Sam cooks a "Shire" meal of stewed rabbit; Sam makes up a little poem about an "Oliphaunt" against the massed shouts and singing of the hoards pouring into the Black Gate; he provides a defense for Frodo in his stability, his courage, his reminder of life in the distant Shire, memory, as it were, alive and well in Mordor. This same gentle stability is impervious to the power of the Ring. When he decides to carry the Ring after Frodo has seemingly been killed by Shelob, Sam feels the pressure of it on him, "gnawing at his will and reason." He feels how great it would be to become Samwise the Strong, Hero of the Age, who would save the world from Sauron with a flaming sword: "He had only to put on the Ring and claim it for his own, and all this could be done.

> In that hour of trial it was the love of his master that helped most to hold him firm; but also deep down in him lived still unconquered his plain hobbit-sense; he knew in the core of his heart that he was not large enough to bear such a burden, even if such visions were not a mere cheat to betray him" (III, 216).

"The love of his master" is genuine feeling for another and a respect for himself which is not slavery or English snobbishness on Tolkien's part but the moral expression of a hierarchical relationship without which the concomitant sense of himself as a gardener would be worthless to Sam. Sam has all the self-awareness necessary to survive and a "core" of love for Frodo which is the finest kind of love because it is "for" someone else, rather than a destructive possessivness. When Frodo falls under Shelob's bite, Sam runs to his rescue, heedless of himself; it is his decision to turn aside from the Quest and go back to save Frodo's body that brings them back together (Frodo is not dead but captured by orcs) and enables the Quest to go on: "My place is by Mr. Frodo.

They must understand that—Elrond and the Council, and the great Lords and Ladies with all their wisdom. Their plans have gone wrong. I can't be their Ring-bearer. Not without Mr. Frodo" (II, 438). His songs and poetry are necessarily simple, described not with condescension on Tolkien's part, but with respect for the servant of others.

Smeagol, on the other hand, has less will and fights a hopeless battle to keep his oath to Frodo. He is necessary to lead the two hobbits over the Dead Marshes, but his passion for the Ring destroys whatever integrity he has. Unlike Sam, the Gollum is not close to Nature in the gardens of the Shire, nor does he have much sense of action motivated by love for another. The hobbits capture him soon after beginning their journey and he promises to guide them to Mordor. Afraid of the elven-made cloaks they wear, and the elven-rope, as evil is afraid of goodness, the Gollum seems to change when once he promises to obey the Ring-bearer: "He spoke with less hissing and whining, and he spoke to his companions direct, not to his precious self" (II, 286). What he misses is the love which the hobbits share, and at a desperate moment on the Stairs of Cirith Ungol, he even makes a gesture of affection to the sleeping Frodo, "almost the touch was a caress," a sign of the weary near-hobbit that he is, "shrunken by the years that had carried him far beyond his time, beyond friends and kin, and the fields and streams of youth, an old starved pitiable thing" (II, 411). He cannot sustain this love: he struggles to keep his promise in a schizophrenic dialogue between his "selves," overheard by Sam, but the pull of the Ring is too strong. If he had it, "Perhaps we grows very strong, stronger than Wraiths. Lord Smeagol? Gollum the Great? *The* Gollum! Eat fish every day, three times a day, fresh from the Sea. Most Precious Gollum!" (II, 304). The humor in this parody of others who might take the Ring (and of human beings who take themselves too seriously) is subordinate finally, to the pain hidden behind this small triumph.

Frodo sees and responds to the Gollum's anguish: when he might kill Smeagol, he does not, remembering that Bilbo had shown the Gollum pity and mercy. "I will not touch the creature. For now that I see him, I do pity him" (II, 281). Frodo feels sympathy for Smeagol because, as Sam observes, he is like him, also a victim of the Ring. But Frodo's decision, evoked by this treacherous outcast, is also a great moral decision, perhaps the most important in *The Lord of the Rings*. It represents a "reaching-out" of the imagination which is based, quite realistically, on Frodo's own desires, but desires transformed by the imagination into a gesture of sympathy in which "possessiveness" is rejected in favor of compassion. In a paradoxical way, the lowest of Middle-earth's creatures, the Gollum, evokes from its highest, the Ring-bearer, that creature's very best response. Frodo's heroism lies not only in his powers of endurance and his willed struggle to destroy the Ring without being destroyed by it. He can also give to others that loving, forgiving respect which created beings can give. Gandalf had told him not to kill the Gollum: ". . . be not too eager to deal out death in the name of justice, fearing for your own safety. Even the wise cannot see all ends." Frodo's compassion spares the wretched creature; not even Sam, for all his naturalness, knows this act of charity in the Christian sense. Like Galadriel or Gandalf, both of whom refuse the Ring, Frodo rejects its corrupting power over another being, and remains himself, even at the cost of his near-destruction.

As it turns out, both Sam and Smeagol are necessary to help in the destruction of the Ring; Frodo's act of mercy "pays off." Tolkien's success here is in the complexity of the end; the Apocalypse, that destruction of the old to permit the new to be born, occurs through the mixed motives and actions of many beings, not those of a single noble hero. Smeagol betrays the hobbits to Shelob who nearly does them in. He flees before Sam's sword, and does not reappear until Frodo and Sam arrive, after many trials, on the slopes of Mt. Doom. Here they are at their last gasp, but determined to go on. Sam's will has "hardened" in him; he feels he was perhaps created only to carry Frodo, which he must often do, to the great furnace of the Cracks of Doom buried in the mountain's side. He feels "as if he was

186

turning into some creature of stone and steel that neither despair nor weariness nor endless barren miles could subdue" (III, 259). At the same time, he gives Frodo all the care he can, holding his hands, kissing him, carrying him on his back. The Gollum reappears, "driven by a devouring desire and a terrible fear," and attacks the pilgrims on the last lap of their journey. Sam cannot bear to hurt him now, he is so miserable. But where the creature has been ruined by his suffering, Frodo has been transformed. Sam sees the two contrasted again, the one crouching, ruined, the other changed by his suffering, "stern, untouchable now by pity, a figure robed in white, but at its breast a wheel of fire" (III, 272). Frodo, in fact, has been stretched beyond his hobbit nature by this point in the Quest; he can never go back to the Shire as he was.

At the last moment, when the salvation of the world depends upon the destruction of the Ring, Frodo cannot bring himself to do it. But on the edge of the Cracks of Doom, as Frodo puts on the Ring, surrendering at last to its pressure, Smeagol attacks once more, bites off Frodo's finger with the Ring on it, and falls into the terrible fires to his, and the Ring's, destruction. In a great burst of noise, flame, and ruin, Sauron's kingdom is destroyed, exactly at the moment the Allies are battling to keep his attention occupied on the Field of Cormallen. Frodo's merciful imaginative gesture toward the suffering Gollum many days before in the Emyn Muil leads to the end of the dead forms created by the Dark Lord; even as the skies burst in rain and lightning, the Nazgûl, directed too late to Mt. Doom, are caught in the destruction and like rockets, "they crackled, withered, and went out." The Will that gave them their only life is subverted by an act of the imagination.

This conclusion to the War of the Ring is in keeping with all that has gone before. Even the smallest creature has a place in the great plan of the universe, and that creature—perhaps a hobbit or even the miserable Gollum himself—must be left to fulfill his destiny and to grow or corrupt as his power permits. Sauron cannot understand the freedom necessary to created beings, and so, as Gandalf suggests, he ignores the hobbits until too late. More importantly, he ignores their "power," which makes them able to love, to suffer, to sacrifice for others as possessed beings cannot. He forgets, too, the fallible character of schemes and schemers, and the importance of chance, of accident in the working out of history. To accomplish the destruction of evil, Frodo has to be himself, to listen to his own nature as it spoke to him in feelings and found expression in action. By expressing pity for the Gollum he leaves that creature free to fulfill his role in history, accidently, inevitably.

Behind this "accidental" conclusion to the Quest lies Tolkien's belief in the efficacy of the moral vision which must work itself out, which *will* work itself out, in the acts and desires of even the simplest beings. The apocalypse is finally an assertion of the tremendously simple nature of essential being expressed through individual events and creatures, the diverse parts of the fragmented world. But when the Maker and the thing Made, the subject and object of the Quest, are reunited, all errors of perception are cleared away, and eternal Nature asserts itself from where it lay hidden behind illusion and disguise. But the magic word cannot be spoken until the long journey of suffering, of trial, of cleansing is gone through; and until the time, beyond any single creature's control, is ready.

Each being helps Middle-earth participate in the process of recovery, that renewal of belief in the imagined world, which is still an ordering of that world. The task of the Ring-bearer and his faithful (and unfaithful) servants is completed: Frodo and Sam, hand in hand, are rescued from the ruins of Mt. Doom by eagles and carried away to their reward, which lies less in any material thing than in their part in renewing the earth and beginning the Age of Men. Again, the events are recorded from their point of view, and the recovery of Middle-earth finds its symbolic form in their "discovery" that Gandalf is still alive, that Aragorn is King Elessar, that pollen from a little box given Sam by Galadriel will make the damaged Shire bloom again. Tolkien's view of life, however, does not permit any simple conclusion to *The Lord of the Rings*:

if the new age is to begin, the old must pass away, and gain must be paid for with destruction. The renewal of the kingdom of men is balanced by the loss to Middle-earth of its heroes like Frodo and Gandalf; comic affirmation and tragic go together.

Aragorn fulfills the Prophecies of the past and returns to the throne of his fathers, a kind of mythical ruler who has proved his worth in trial and battle, and now represents the Community in its perfected political form, ruled by virtue. King Elessar returns the symbolic Eldest of Trees, sacred to the ruling line, to Minas Tirith; he marries the daughter of the elven prince, Elrond; he brings together in his own person the powers of war and healing. His renewed strength is symbolized by Tolkien in the renewal of the ancient city itself. Minas Tirith is from the start set against Minas Morgol, the black city of Sauron, which promises only death to its inhabitants. But Minas Tirith is in the apocalyptic tradition which identifies the Kingdom of Jesus with His city. In the *Book of Revelation*, St. John has a vision of a "new heaven and a new earth" which are to appear after the defeat of the forces of evil. And the manifestation of the renewal of life is the new Jerusalem, the City of God, in which the Holy Spirit is to dwell forever.

The image of the city is a metaphor for civilization, for the ordered preservation of the constructions of the imagination, a "work of art" in Tolkien's sense. The river of life flows through it; on its banks grows the tree of life; and all those souls who are saved may enter into the city at its open gates, with their right to the tree and its fruits (*Revelation*, chaps. 21–22). The Bible promises no division between the city and the natural world, between God and man, for "the tabernacle of God is with men, and they shall be his people" (*Rev.* 21:3). But this is a vision promised to St. John at the Second Coming of Christ. At the end of *The Lord of the Rings* the natural divisions between heaven and earth are not destroyed but reaffirmed. King Elessar rules over Minas Tirith rebuilt, in which there is a mixture of created things and natural life. It serves as the capital city for Middle-earth which is itself renewed, the gardens of Ithilien blooming again. The City is not the construction of stone and jewels described in *Revelation* but a combination of organic and created substance in which the necessary rule of power, imaginatively employed, continues. Aragorn takes on the qualities of the mythic kings who are not only wise warriors, but are also symbolic of reproduction and new life, the fertility of their people:

> In his time the City was made more fair than it had ever been, even in the days of its first glory; and it was filled with trees and with fountains, and its gates were wrought of mithril and steel, and its streets were paved with white marble; and the Folk of the Mountain laboured in it, and the Folk of the Wood rejoiced to come there; and all was healed and made good, and the houses were filled with men and women and the laughter of children, and no window was blind nor any courtyard empty; and after the ending of the Third Age of the world into the new age it preserved the memory and the glory of the years that were gone (III, 304).

The Fourth Age must be wisely ruled, as expressive of the imagination's power as it can be, and the wise king must continue it and defend it, not falling back upon custom for its own sake, nor forgetting the need for vigilance against the future rise of evil, inevitable, alas, with the passage of time. And the rebirth of joyous life in Minas Tirith, the City of God on earth, is the inevitable consequence of recovery, the "regaining of a clear view." But this is still not the perfect unity of heaven; history goes on.

Aragorn's Quest ends in renewal and recovery; and so does Frodo's, with the difference that the Ring-bearer—wounded by evil, stretched beyond his nature by his struggle to preserve that nature—can no longer remain among his kind in Middle-earth. With Arwen's gift to him of her immortality, he must pass into the West with the Eternal Ones. This is the paradoxical reward for the Hero: Frodo has saved Middle-earth, preserving its homely beauty as he has known it, for others, but has lost it for himself. The beauty of Tolkien's conclusion to the Trilogy lies in the ironic but inevitable combination of gain and loss which occurs in history, in growth, in Recovery itself.

The renewal of the larger world is duplicated in the "Cleansing of the Shire" which the hobbits must conduct on their return, for Sauron has contaminated even that placid pastoral backwater, and the warriors return home not to peace but to continued warfare. The Shire has been invaded by the debased Saruman and his hirelings, who cut down the trees, tear up the rural communities, put in a giant mill to pollute the air and water, and establish a police state in a vest-pocket parody of the Dark Lord's dominion. As in the larger world, the enemy is driven out with warfare, the Battle of Bywater being the last engagement ever fought in the Shire. But it is a real battle; nearly seventy "ruffians lay dead on the field." Frodo does not fight, but tries to prevent the hobbits "in their wrath at their losses, from slaying those of their enemies who threw down their weapons." This is another instance of Tolkien's realistic view of human experience: passion, hate, destructive wrath are not good; but they are part of the make-up of created beings, and are not to be kept out of fairy-stories. Strong feeling can be useful, and needs to be controlled, not repressed.

But once the Shire has been "scoured," renewed but not altered, Sam takes on the mythic stature of his gardener's role, and like a hobbit-Johnny Appleseed, scatters the pollen given him by Galadriel over the countryside. He "gives" to everyone and to Nature itself, where the builders of mill and quarry had sought to "take" and give nothing in return. Trees are planted again, the mill torn down, the stream cleansed. This is not merely an idyllic dream; everyone in the Shire works at effecting Recovery, making it manifest in the world around them. Shaken out of their possessiveness and fear, the hobbits "realize imagined wonder" with their own hands. That year there is "wonderful sunshine and delicious rain, in due times and perfect measure"; there is an "air of richness and growth"; children born in that year have rich golden hair; and strawberries abound; "and no one was ill, and everyone was pleased . . ." (III, 375). This is the tradition of Man working with Nature to preserve Nature's abundance, and his. This is the "great creating nature" of Shakespeare's *The Winter's Tale,* the story of lost children recovered, and belief as a guide to truth sustained. In that play Nature and Man the Gardener are allied as "artists," working together to fertilize and renew. Sam himself marries, and begets children, thus performing at his level the parallel function of the folk hero, King Elessar, at his. In the agrarian world from which our myths are drawn, the fertility of the earth is coincident with that of man, the productivity of the latter ensuring the former. At the end of *The Winter's Tale,* King Leontes is reunited with his "lost" daughter and his "dead" wife, and the renewal of his ability to believe in love and hope finds its form in the reunion of his family. Some great myths end happily, and represent this happiness in the return to unity of dispersed or fragmented members. What we see of this in *The Lord of the Rings* represents that eucatastrophe of which Tolkien writes in "On Fairy-Stories." In the recovery of life, in the reunion of families, in the assertion that joy is possible to hobbits and to us, we see, in little, that larger Joy which Tolkien defines as Christian and eternal, expressed in the Great Eucatastrophe of Christ. "Art has been verified. God is the Lord, of angels, and of men— and of elves. Legend and History have met and fused" ("On Fairy-Stories," 72).

The final test is in our own response to Tolkien's fairy-story. Like Adam, Sam the Gardener remains behind to care for the Shire, and govern it because hobbits (and as yet fallen Men) still need governing. But Frodo is now "stretched" beyond his nature, and departs in pain, for the Grey Havens. The price he must pay for his heroism is to be an outcast from the society he saved: "It must often be so, Sam, when things are in danger: some one has to give them up, lose them, so that others may keep them" (III, 382). Like Bilbo, Frodo signals his end by becoming an historian, continuing that seminal work, *The Downfall of the Lord of the Rings and the*

Return of the King. He gives the manuscript to Sam, a gesture to the future, and then rides with Bilbo, the high elves, and Gandalf from their beloved Middle-earth forever. The somber conclusion on the quay, when Frodo must say farewell to Sam and leave this world, is extraordinarily moving. Like ghosts, the departing ones move through the familiar Shire to the Havens, already transcendent, legendary beings who have passed beyond history into myth. Self-made works of art, they can converse without speech, from mind to mind: "only their shining eyes stirred and kindled as their thoughts went to and fro" (III, 325).

In William Blake's sense, Frodo and the others have become metaphors, entering literally into the eternal imaginative vision that is reality. Tolkien relies heavily here upon the wealth of Western myth representing death and transfiguration: the unseen company of spiritual beings; the vision of the Eternal Lands to which they go; the eternal regret for earth and its beauty which they must surrender. The White Ship is like many ships from *Beowulf* to the legends of King Arthur which bear away fallen but immortal heroes. Even Cirdan the Shipwright is like Charon, the ferryman across the Styx, who guides the boat to its destination with its cargo of souls. But also unlike, for Tolkien's art forces us to award Secondary Belief not to the familiar figures of classical myth but to elves and hobbits. Our tears are not only for the loss to us of friends to whom we have been so close. They are also for their transfiguration as a triumphant consequence of the Quest, now fulfilled. Frodo does not become another being with a different nature; he is elevated to become one with Elendil who "voyaged alone" in elvish legend and was translated to a place among the stars. But his legend takes life from Frodo's repetition of it. We *feel* that what has happened is *true*; we *believe* in it through the imaginative response the tale has evoked in us. And our tears are not just for loss, but for the Joy which even loss can affirm.

Frodo and the hobbits have become legend. Tolkien furthers this within the story by noting that Sam and Frodo see themselves as "being in a tale" in the process of being told. In a terrible moment on their way to the Stairs of Cirith Ungol, the hobbits crouch in a dark crevice and as they share what "they expected would be their last meal," Sam develops a theory about their condition based on his experience. He points out that his idea of "adventures" has changed. Before he had seen them as something folk in the stories "went out and looked for, because they were exciting and life was a bit dull, a kind of a sport, as you might say" (II, 407). But he has found, instead, that "folk" are "landed" in adventures; "their paths were laid that way." And those who survive are those "as just went on," who stuck it out, enduring evil. He wonders what kind of a tale he and Frodo have fallen into. Frodo answers that they cannot know: real tales do not appear to their participants as "happy-ending or sad-ending," only to those who hear the story afterward. Frodo seems to suggest here that all of us are in "tales" though we do not know this; like the hobbits we are creatures of legend. For Sam suddenly realizes that he and Frodo are in a tale, after all, that begun by the hero Beren, who "never thought he was going to get that Silmaril from the Iron Crown in Thangorodrim, and yet he did, and that was a worse place and a blacker danger than ours." In this simple way, he notes that the tale "goes on past the happiness and into grief and beyond it" (II, 407–8). And these are the tales worth listening to. Time is recorded in terms of the suffering beings who live in it. But they are also "recording" it through their adventures, and seen this way, adventures have meaning, become Art, demand Belief which short-circuits Time's destructive force. The hobbits' discovery that they are in a story must also throw us, as readers, into that dislocation of reality (which is truth and which fiction?) that evokes an imaginative response. After all, Sam and Frodo are in the next chapter of Beren's Tale. And we in the next: ". . . and the Silmaril went on and came to Earendil. And why, sir, I never thought of that before! We've got— you've got some of the light of it in that star-glass that the Lady gave you! Why, to think of it, we're in the same tale still! It's going on. Don't the great tales never end?"

Conclusion: The Realization of Wonder

If we compare Tolkien to other contemporary writers, we see major differences. Unlike such writers of fantasy as Kurt Vonnegut, Tolkien is never crudely satiric; gentleness and love pervade his work and soften the criticism of modern society implicit in it. Where other authors present a bleak picture of the wasteland in which the soul struggles to survive alone, Tolkien gives us the Fellowship of the Ring as a happier alternative, a small society of loving creatures who are not alone in the universe. Tolkien argues that there is much of value in Western culture which should be saved, which *will* be saved, by the imaginative beings who have power to believe in themselves. Tolkien is a conservative in this sense; for all the elements of the fantastic in his work, the preservation of traditional values is most important to him. The fantastic affirms those values rather than attempting to substitute something else for them. Tolkien's writing style, too, is not meant to surprise or shock us; it is always subordinate to the story being told. It is his retelling of our most deeply believed myths about ourselves that makes *The Lord of the Rings* so moving.

Tolkien is read because he tells a good story; his power to command Secondary Belief in his readers is real. History comes alive in the characters and events of *The Lord of the Rings* because Tolkien creates speeches and actions which have the "inner consistency of reality" and are not absolutely and destructively rooted in the "observed fact" of the Primary World. He has chosen to tell a story, rather than write a philosophic discourse, and this decision was important because a narrative presents "inner" reality in a way a discursive essay does not: imagined beings who take their life from the hands of their creator touch our emotions, our imaginations, our religious sense of wonder, in ways words addressed to the intellect alone cannot. As William Blake wrote long ago, we cannot really imagine God as a cloud; we must imagine Him in the form most meaningful to us, that of a man. Men, or created beings of other races, act enough like men in Tolkien's fantasies, to remind us that we, too, progress through time toward death; that we, too, love life and fear evil. And in this way the fantastic in its narrative form comes closer to representing that total body of knowledge and being which is ourself more than many other literary kinds. In order to make this happen, the fantasist gives us actions and shapes which seem familiar; but he also frees us from dependency upon "observed fact" so that the imagination can work and our vision of the unknown world can show us new things in ourselves.

Behind Tolkien's choice of form lies an assumption about the nature of man which shines through his work: that men can love, admire good deeds, can seek truth because it is good. They are not "bad"; they are imperceptive, they are weak insofar as excessive self-pride makes them misuse their particular powers; they are available, however, to correction, to change, to the Power, used only for good, of the Enchanter. Words and literary forms are not things apart from human beings. They come up from the body and the feelings attached to the Primary World, as they are, and they share in that reality. And much more. The "Joy" of which Tolkien writes in "On Fairy-Stories" is "heavenly" all right, but it underlies the events in *The Lord of the Rings*, too, in the "turn" of the happy ending, and in the life of the narration itself.

This is important because we also read Tolkien for other reasons which come through to us because of his way of presenting them. Tolkien has gone against the present style of literary fashion; he does not give us the private rhetoric of the symbolist or the inner-directed world of the despairing self-analyst whose psychological conflicts spin out a novel's length. Rather than make a meaningful world out of an individual's isolated and particular nature, he returns to the myths of the past and to the mythic story of the Quest in which all men can share. This argues for the universal significance of experience and so for the pervasive moral effects of the imagination. Individual suffering and bewilderment reveal valuable meaning in a mythic context; nor is suffering exceptional and meaningful only to the individual. If as Mark Schorer says, myths are images "that give philosophical meaning to the facts of ordinary life," then a writer of myth writes for his whole society as well as every individual who suffers and imagines in it. Fantasy is not escape in the sense of flight from reality, Tolkien reminds us, but an affirmation of man's ability to order reality, a schema for handling the problems which power creates, for "realizing imagined wonder." His success at reconstituting the fairy-story for the twentieth century lies in part in his sense of our moral necessities.

Another reason for reading Tolkien is his assertion that the Imagination has value in the Primary World. For many people, growing up in a culture which seems to emphasize the uniformity of lives on the assembly line or in split-level suburbs, works of fantasy must be suspect because they represent imagined existence and exceptional beings. Tolkien shows throughout *The Hobbit* and *The Lord of the Rings* that we can be surprised by our fellows: the hobbits of the Shire perform heroic feats we would never have expected. But it is this unexpected quality of the imagination, popping up when least expected, that readers must find attractive, especially since this power for good solves problems, directs actions, opens up possibilities in Tolkien's fantasies. And for readers who resist the homogeneity and conformity of contemporary life, there is appeal in the variety of imagined beings— elves, dwarves, ents, hobbits—who appear in the hills and valleys of Middle-earth. Not only the profusion of races, but the respect which they can show to each other must be important for Americans perplexed by racial segregation, sexual discrimination, xenophobia and their divisive, hate-engendering effects. In *The Lord of the Rings*, we find a Fellowship, a United Nations, based upon commons needs and shared affection, even between the most disparate peoples. The fight against "possessiveness," the possibilities of "Recovery," are happy alternatives in a possessive society.

In Tolkien's world, respect is paid not only to other "races" but to living things generally. Perhaps the most important problem in the latter half of the twentieth century is presented by the natural environment, ravaged by possessive men in search of wealth and power. In the Trilogy, the evil beings are connected with such desecration; Saruman and Sauron both attack the natural organic world, leveling forests, covering vegetation with ash-piles,

factories and their waste, the "produce" of slave-worked mines. But those who fight against evil respect the natural world, as guardians of all created beings. The ents care for their trees, the dwarves for their gleaming minerals. Aragorn finds help for wounds in the *athelas*, a wild herb. Sam grows an elven tree, the *Mallorn*, far from its home in Lorien. The imagination requires that even plants be permitted their own natures, and shown care rather than possessiveness. This general respect for all created life in *The Lord of the Rings* speaks to those among us who fear the disappearance of redwoods and whales, mountain wilderness and hidden seashores to serve society's destructive needs. If we try to turn every mountain valley into a national park with camping areas, general stores and play grounds, we have remade it in our image, and so extended a step further "the drab blur of triteness or familiarity" which must ultimately threaten our own necessary sense of wonder at other forms of life. And under our heavy hand, such unique life can be extinguished. *Care for the world*, might be the theme of Tolkien's Trilogy.

Nor does the Imagination deny the existence of evil. Our society can be accused of hiding reality under its images: the glossy prints of the large-circulation magazines or the smiling caricatures of housewives discovering a new soap in television commercials. Distress is smoothed away, and suffering denied not only existence but value. People hurt, however; they suffer from poverty, hunger, loneliness, fear and a long list of human symptoms which no soap product or movie star can cure. They also suffer from the absence of great causes for which to suffer, paradoxical as that may seem. In Tolkien's fantasy, we do not escape from evil: there is no running away from the Shadow of Sauron. The ways in which created beings respond to the challenge such power presents distinguish them; make them more complex in nature than we think at first; make them moral. For a reader tired of seeing human beings as only partial figures caught in the conventions of social life and prescribed rituals, the revelation of hidden natures available for good or evil is valuable.

And, finally, beyond its social implications, the imagination in its guise of the fantastic, separate from "observed fact," gives life to the world in a way the sciences, the academic disciplines which emphasize reason or mathematical formulae, do not. As man begins to discover more and more about the laws which govern life, and seems to be reducing life to equations tested in a laboratory, our human response is to seek the unreasonable, the irrational, feelings and visions which may be condemned by the scientist because they cannot be analyzed or represented statistically. Love, responsibility, and will power cannot be computed, yet they exist, and seem to have much more to do with human conduct than laws and figures. The appeal of fantasy implies instinctive rejection of what seems impersonal, unfeeling, insensitive to our human desires, in the century of nuclear bombs, germ warfare, and government policy beyond the power of any individual to influence.

In fact, Tolkien emphasizes feeling in *The Lord of the Rings*. Characters not only develop love for one another, they express it in companionship, in sacrifice, in loyalty. They show it by kissing and holding hands. They respond to their feelings by expressing anger or love. They have strong responses to events, and make decisions based on such feelings. Suffering, looked upon as an evil in a society which does not have a religious context in which to understand and accept it, is feeling which draws characters together in Tolkien and alters their vision of the world and of themselves. To confront anguish or pain in life—rather than repressing it and denying its existence—is a step toward reality.

But the value of strong feeling as a causal element speaks to another point in Tolkien's work: the emphasis upon the individual and his ability to *do* something, to make things happen, even against what seem enormous odds. Part of the boredom which men experience in modern society comes from feeling that there is nothing worthwhile they can do to express themselves as individuals. After a day at the office, shuffling papers, we turn to expensive cars, drink or casual sex to give us a sense of purpose and value which the ordinary round of life does not provide. But these interests are not enough to really satisfy that wish to be "meaningful" which commitment to a larger social or spiritual purpose can give. In Tolkien's fantasy, we can see that under imaginative direction, action is possible. Men and hobbits make decisions and then take steps to fulfill them. Feeling and ideas are not bottled up and finally reduced to dreams, but lead to changes, realizations of vision, which imaginative created beings may direct. The quests of Frodo and Aragorn are a series of events in which the Hero chooses and performs.

Not that all actions have to glorious. Part of the sympathy we feel for Frodo and Sam, who "act" heroically in their journey through Mordor, may come from our sense that to endure and be patient is all we can do. Frodo's heroism does not lie in his warrior's abilities (which are small) or his command of men. It lies in his commitment to a greater vision of life than himself, and it is his dogged plodding through the dispiriting wastes that makes him so significant. The justification for his heroism lies in the larger purposes he fulfills as Ring-bearer. We sympathize with his loneliness, his desparation, but we see he completes the designs of a universal plan, indeed, is the most important element in that plan. We may feel no such plan exists for us, but neither was Frodo very sure; his persistence in his quest is made in spite of, perhaps because of, this uncertainty, a willed affirmation of his own value. Frodo *puts* value in the universe, through his own efforts, and it is in this heroic act that we may find the positive analogy for our lives in the Primary World.

We should also remember that Frodo's self-sacrifice is not only for the defeat of evil; it is also for the good of society, for the whole Community of created beings. This suggests, in turn, that in the mind of the fantasist, society is worth saving. It is not a mechanical horror designed to grind the individual down. Instead, personal commitment —*service*—is honored by the citizens of Middle-earth. The individual finds a responsible place for himself in his society; those who live outside society are identified with tyranny and self-destruction. A major reason for Tolkien's popularity among students and the "rebellious young" may be his classic insistence that the individual finds true freedom in the service of good, and that good can be social, providing security and purpose for others without being destructive of singularity and wilfullness.

Behind Tolkien's work, in other words, we can find a deeply religious commitment to Western culture and its values, ragged and unsatisfactory as they may seem to some of us. But Tolkien's use, in his major work, of our most pervasive myths—the Quest, the sacrifice of the god for the renewal of life, the battle of good and evil—

suggests that he does not feel we have come so far from our origins that art and life, fantasy and human needs, are far apart. That he chose to cast his story in the Middle-earth of an earlier age with a set of characters whom we may or may not have met before, argues for his faith in our imagination and our ability to believe. We must be able to want to realize "imagined wonder" in spite of the Primary World in which we also live. That we read *The Lord of the Rings* with tears and love argues for his success: we are willing to believe in this form of the myth of our life. Like the Christian myth which underlies Tolkien's view of experience in the twentieth century, the myth of the War of the Ring gives emotional and spiritual meaning to much of what we know. It, too, affirms the grandest moral purposes of the universe, and asserts that there are ultimate values in which we may believe. As Thomas Carlyle put it almost one hundred and fifty years ago, in a century when values seemed as problematic as in this one: "The Universe is not dead and demoniacal, a charnel-house with spectres; but godlike, and my Father's!" [21] Belief is not just faith in a church doctrine; it is a commitment to a meaningful reality and to our ability to believe in ourselves. For *The Lord of the Rings* is a "joyful" book; and its happy ending is not the only source of that knowledge. We read it with delight because it makes us feel that pleasure, and thus it tells us not only that the universe is godlike but that we are, too. Tolkien can be accused of sentimentality, but this is not always a pejorative epithet. Feeling which reunites lovers, discovers lost children or parents, returns the wanderer to his long-abandoned home—feeling has an honorable place in the structure of the imagination, and our response to Tolkien's myth is an honest guide to our own—and society's—reality.

Bibliography:

These are the editions of Tolkien's works used in this study:

The Lord of the Rings. 3 vols. New York: Ballantine Books, 1965.

The Hobbit. New York: Ballantine Books, 1966.

The Tolkien Reader. New York: Ballantine Books, 1966.

This is the best collection of critical essays on Tolkien:

Isaacs, Neil D., and Rose A. Zimbardo, eds. *Tolkien and the Critics.* Notre Dame: University of Notre Dame Press, 1969.

These books provide background for a study of Tolkien:

Beowulf. Translated by Burton Raffel. New York: Mentor Books, 1963.

Campbell, Joseph. *The Hero with a Thousand Faces.* Princeton: Princeton University Press, 1949.

———————————— *The Masks of God*. 3 vols. New York: Viking Press, 1959–64.

Carter, Lin. *Tolkien: A Look Behind "The Lord of the Rings."* New York: Ballantine Books, 1969.

Frazer, James G. *The Golden Bough*. New York: The Mac-Millan Co., 1927.

Frye, Northrop. *Anatomy of Criticism*. Princeton: Princeton University Press, 1957.

Morris, William. *The Well at the World's End*. 2 vols. New York: Ballantine Books, 1970.

Sir Gawain and the Green Knight. New York: Holt, Rinehart and Winston, 1964.

Spenser, Edmund. *The Faerie Queene*, in *The Poetical Works of Edmund Spenser*, edited by J.C. Smith and E. deSelincourt. London: Oxford University Press, 1942.

Footnotes:

[1] Robert Langbaum, *The Poetry of Experience* (New York: W.W. Norton, 1963), p.137.

[2] William Blake, *Complete Writings*, edited by Geoffrey Keynes (London: Oxford University Press, 1966), p.151.

[3] Blake, p.150.

[4] "On Fairy-Stories," in *The Tolkien Reader* (New York: Ballantine Books, 1966), p.47. Further references are to this edition and will be identified in the text.

[5] Foreword to *The Lord of the Rings* (New York: Ballantine Books, 1965), I, viii. Further references to *The Lord of the Rings* are to this edition and will be identified by volume number and page in the text.

[6] Northrop Frye, *Anatomy of Criticism* (Princeton: Princeton University Press, 1957), p.94.

[7] Blake, "A Vision of the Last Judgment," p.611.

[8] Mark Schorer, *William Blake: The Politics of Vision* (New York: Vintage Books, 1959), p.25.

[9] Philip Wheelwright, quoted by Schorer, p.26.

[10] William Morris, *The Well at the World's End* (New York: Ballantine Books, 1970), I, 11.

[11] *The Hobbit* (New York: Ballantine Books, 1966), p.76. Further references are to this edition and will be identified in the text.

[12] Morris, I, 210.

[13] "*Beowulf*: The Monster and the Critics," *Proceedings of the British Academy*, XXII (1936), 18.

[14] *Beowulf*, translated by Burton Raffel (New York: Mentor Books, 1963), 11. 632–8.

[15] In "Tolkien and Frodo Baggins," Roger Sale discusses the theme of possessiveness in *The Lord of the Rings* (in *Tolkien and the Critics*, edited by Neil Isaacs and Rose A. Zimbardo [Notre Dame: University of Notre Dame Press, 1969], p. 264). This is the single most important essay yet written on the Trilogy, and I owe a great deal to Professor Sale's comments on point of view and style.

[16] Rose A. Zimbardo, "Moral Vision in *The Lord of the Rings*," in *Tolkien and the Critics*, p.101.

[17] Zimbardo discusses the importance of the will in her instructive essay (pp.100–108). See also Patricia Meyer Spacks, "Power and Meaning in *The Lord of the Rings*," in *Tolkien and the Critics*, pp.81–99. She points out the importance of responsibility and a sense of cosmic order in Tolkien's world.

[18] Sale, pp.247f.

[19] Sale, p.259.

[20] Zimbardo, p.100.

[21] Thomas Carlyle, "The Everlasting Yea," *Sartor Resartus* (New York: Doubleday, Doran & Co., 1937), p.188.

HERMANN HESSE

by Edwin F. Casebeer

Throughout his long career, Nobel Prize winning author Hermann Hesse struggled heroically, in his life and works, with some of the central questions of our age.

In **Hermann Hesse,** Edwin F. Casebeer brings out Hesse's amazing breadth of subjects, situations, characters, themes, techniques, and shows the underlying unity in Hesse's major works.

(68-965) $1.50

available wherever paperbacks are sold